BUSINESS
COOKERY

Tried and tested recipes for business success

Hannah McNamara and Patrick White

Published by HRM Global Ltd
Delta House
175-177 Borough High Street
London SE1 1HR United Kingdom
Telephone: 020 7939 9910
Email: books@hrmglobal.co.uk
Web: www.hrmglobal.co.uk

A CIP catalogue record for this book is available
from the British Library.

ISBN 978 0 9568682 0 6

Dedication

To my wife Michelle for accompanying me on the journey and to my Sungold colleagues Stacey, Ross, Noel and Karen who made a truly great team.
Patrick White

To my wonderful parents and mentors. To my father who taught me independence and inner strength, and to my mother who passed on her gift with words.
Hannah McNamara

About the Authors

Hannah McNamara

A former corporate Head of Marketing, Hannah McNamara changed career and started her own business in 2004. In the years since re-training as an Executive Coach she has become one of the most respected professionals in her field. Her debut business book 'Niche Marketing for Coaches' published in 2007 remains a popular handbook for both new and established coaches alike and she has helped thousands of coaches to start and build their own businesses.

She is a popular conference and seminar speaker on marketing and entrepreneurship. Her articles on leadership, management, negotiation skills and marketing have been published by a variety of magazines and online publications.

She is an in-demand coach working with senior level executives and has an impressive track record in transforming mediocre operational managers into high performing business leaders.

Patrick White

After a successful international corporate career in a variety of industries across 13 countries with responsibilities for up to 14,000 staff Patrick then went on to become a serial entrepreneur owning 14 different businesses in the hospitality, retail, distribution, IT and food and beverage industries. His last business had a turnover of $US 2.0 billion and 600 full-time staff and numerous part-time staff.

For the last 23 years while owning the above businesses, he has also worked as a high level management consultant and Executive Coach in various business and not-for-profit sectors as well as an international public speaker and trainer on a variety of business and people management topics.

Patrick also acts as mentor to many small and medium-sized businesses and entrepreneurs helping them to establish or grow their existing business. He continues to deliver regular public and in-house training seminars and speak at international conferences. Recently he has worked in Switzerland, United Kingdom, Italy, Czech Republic, Ukraine, Russia, Malaysia, Singapore, Australia, Sudan, Oman, Kuwait, Saudi Arabia, Libya, Iran, Qatar, United Arab Emirates and Bahrain. Patrick has also published various articles and papers on Business Strategy, Negotiation Skills, Influencing and Persuading, Emotional Intelligence in the Workplace, Sales and Marketing and issues around Training.

Preface

You may ask why write a business book and use the title "Business Cookery." Well the answer is really quite simple. We were presenting a seminar together which was about practical techniques the attendees could use to get more clients and grow their business. During the course of the seminar we were both unintentionally using cooking analogies to emphasize various points. It was noticeable that when we did so they seemed "to get it." It was also noticeable that after a while the attendees were using cooking analogies themselves to make various points. Obviously the metaphor of cooking was useful to them in understanding business issues. The next question is what could we do with this knowledge? Again the answer was simple. Put it in a book and here we are.

This book is an attempt to impart some wisdom from two people who have not only succeeded in the corporate world but have owned and operated 18+ successful businesses between them. It is not prescriptive and in no way tries to present a particular business model that should be implemented by the reader. Our philosophy is simple and applies to employees as well as entrepreneurs. It is that in nearly all cases success is usually the result of hard work and the application of wisdom. If we can help a little in providing you with the getting of wisdom we will have succeeded.

Business Cookery

The awkward silence on the phone line was making her anxious. "It's alright darling, you can tell me what's wrong," said Barbara. "Have you and Simon had a fight?"

"Oh Mum, it's just awful," Jenny tried her hardest to hold back the tears. They came anyway. "How could they do this to me? I've known them for years."

"Jenny, why don't you tell me what's happened? Maybe I can help." She could hear her daughter was hurting. All she wanted to do was give her a cuddle. Even at 39 daughters still need their mums, especially when they are hundreds of miles away.

"I spent ages planning a black-tie dinner party for my birthday. It was supposed to be a get-together for all the girls from school." Her voice trembled as she continued. "I've just been on Facebook and everyone's making excuses why they can't come. Some of them haven't said one way or the other and the party's only a few days away. I know they've all got kids and commitments, but surely they can make a Tuesday night."

Barbara sighed gently in a fruitless attempt to soothe her daughter's pain. She gave Jenny a moment to dry her eyes before speaking. "Darling, before your father and I sold the agency and moved we used to put on a lot of dinner parties for clients. I know you probably don't want to hear this but we never had anyone not show up or pull out at the last minute. Something must have gone wrong if *no one's* coming."

"Well," Jenny said indignantly, "I've been so busy with the business; I can't just drop everything for a party. I've been working on it when I can. I got my assistant to help me planning the food and getting recipes together. She's ordered new tablecloths, sorted out the music, ordered fresh flowers, put it on Facebook... I don't see what else I could have done."

"What about the invitations? When did you send them out?" asked Barbara.

"It's on Facebook," said Jenny.

"I realize that. What I mean is when did you start inviting people?" said Barbara.

"I think she set it up as an event on Monday," said Jenny.

Barbara was sure she'd misunderstood, but wanted to check, "what - *this* Monday?"

"Yes."

For what seemed like an eternity, the crackling of the phone line was the only sign Barbara had that the call was still connected.

"Mum, you're right. I should have given people more notice. If someone invited me to something next week, I wouldn't be able to make it either. I'm rushing from one thing to the next. I've had to stop going to that evening class because Simon can't get back from his office in time to take the kids off my hands. I feel like such a mess right now. Mum what should I do?"

Instinctively Barbara cradled the phone between her head and shoulder and rolled up her sleeves. "If there's one thing I learned from building the agency it's how to get people to come to an event. Grab a pen Jenny and I'll tell you how to do it."

Exactly 37 minutes later they hung up the phone and Jenny looked down at her notes. She knew what she had in front of her wasn't just the plan for running a dinner party, it was the strategy she sorely needed for turning around her ailing business.

FOOD FOR THOUGHT...

Knowledge versus Wisdom

There are many sources of information on how to start, run and grow a business whether it is small, medium or large.

So why are there not many more successful businesses given the wide range of resources that are available to prospective and existing business owners and managers? The reason is that having knowledge does not automatically give you the necessary wisdom that is required to run a successful business.

Knowledge is that which we have learned by observation, experience or learning. How we apply that knowledge, or how we use it for the benefit of others is called wisdom

Another way of expressing it is that knowledge is what you know; wisdom is the capacity to judge. *Wisdom* is knowing what to know, how much and what to do with it. *Knowledge* is obtained, wisdom is developed.

The question is "Can you use your knowledge properly if you have no wisdom?" We think the answer is **no**. You need to *develop* your wisdom.

Running a business requires a continuing set of judgments to be made. Decisions such as who will be our customers, what will we charge, how do we manage employees and so on. There are no set formulas, business models or short cuts that will instantly provide that wisdom.

The story in this book is about two people who build their wisdom to help them be successful.

Chapter 1

As Simon stood poised at the top of the staircase, he felt part superdad, part ninja.

Superdad because Friday was the night he made absolutely sure he got away from work on time so he could put Noah and Rosie to bed and read them a story. It was Jenny's night off to catch up with her Mum Barbara who had moved to Spain with Simon's father-in-law John.

Ninja because cat-like flexibility was needed to get past the two consecutive creaking steps so he didn't risk waking the children.

"Yes!" he thought. "Jet Li eat your heart out," as he successful avoided the noisy obstacles.

He stood triumphantly in the doorway of the lounge, hands on hips. "Kids have had their bath, each had a story and they're asleep. Time to relax for the weekend."

For a moment Jenny giggled to herself, picturing him with cape flowing and of course, his underpants on the outside.

Simon noticed the laptop on the coffee table and the TV on mute. What he didn't notice was the pile of tear-soaked tissues which had almost dried.

"So, how many are coming on Tuesday night?" He sat on the arm of the sofa and it took just one sideways glance from Jenny to remind him if he didn't move quickly, he'd be in for a telling off about how sofa arms aren't that strong, how we're still paying for the sofa and how he shouldn't set a bad example for the children. He moved.

With her husband sat beside her, Jenny explained what had happened on the phone, "Mum's given me some great advice. I've decided to postpone the party a few weeks to a date everyone can make."

"How come?" Simon knew how much work she had already put into organizing it and what it meant to her to have her friends around her.

Since she started her interior design business from home last year, she had hardly seen her old friends. Instead she spent every opportunity meeting new people at local networking events and building her collection of business cards. Getting a freelance PA to handle her paperwork and appointments had been a blessing. It allowed Jenny to focus on what she was good at – design.

"Mum started off by telling me how to organize a dinner party, but as she was talking I realized this was the way she built up the agency with Dad. Here, I've made some notes; I'll talk you through them."

It didn't take long for Jenny to bring Simon up to date. She was expecting an enthusiastic reception so was surprised when he got up and walked out of the room.

"I hate it when you do that," she said under her breath in a barely audible whisper.

She heard the fridge door open, the clink of glasses and the feint pop of the cork leaving the bottle.

Simon set the bottle of wine down on the table and began to pour a glass for each of them. The *glug, glug, glug* of the first wine flowing into the glass was the sound of the working week ending and a hectic weekend of swimming, children's parties and food shopping beginning. She put it out of her mind.

Simon looked thoughtful. "You know, I think this plan of your Mum's could work in my company too."

Simon had recently been appointed Managing Director of a growing software company and had been feeling the pressure to lead the organization to bigger and better things. As an external hire, he sensed the barriers going up from day one. It took only a few days to learn that the influential and charismatic sales director had applied for his position three months previously and hadn't been successful.

"That first step, 'start with your why' reminds me of something I read in 'The 7 Habits of Highly Effective People' by Stephen R. Covey – start with the end in mind. The *why* is the reason the company exists. The Vision and Mission."

He got up and walked out of the room again. Jenny rolled her eyes and took a sip of the ice cold white wine.

Simon came back a few minutes later brandishing a folder. The sofa bounced as he sat down next to her excitedly.

"I kept this from a course I went on at my old company." He flicked through the pages until he found what he was looking for. "This is it. 'Setting your Vision, Mission and Goals'. I've been so wrapped up in the politics and learning about the new company that I hadn't thought to refer to this. This is going to help us set ours. We can do this for your company and mine. That way we'll each know what we're trying to achieve and we can support each other."

Jenny liked the sound of this. It was like the old days. They used to talk about everything and dream for the future, but life had got in the way recently.

That's what had been missing, their *why*. A sense of purpose. Something bigger than them, the kids and the mortgage.

As they started working through the course notes, she felt the flush of adrenalin through her body. "We're onto something now, I can feel it!"

Recipe for Vision & Mission

The Vision and Mission are part of the staple diet of every business. Just like bread they are best baked at home where the aroma conveys warmth and a sense of family to every room.

Of course it's possible to buy mass-produced bread and it's possible to copy the vision and mission of other companies. You will get something off the shelf which does the job, but looks and feels the same as everyone else's.

Equally you could buy a bread-making machine and you could delegate creation of the vision and mission to someone, outside the company - perhaps your marketing agency. It could take a while before they know how to make bread just the way you like it.

It's much more satisfying making it yourself (and you know exactly what's in it!)

Ingredients:
Flour, water, yeast, sugar, salt

Preparation:
Wash your hands – you need to focus so cleanse your mind of thoughts about other work or anything else which needs doing.

Clear a space – get rid of the clutter and distractions, this includes any friction between you and any colleagues. You need to be fully present and engaged to do this properly. Have a clean and clear working environment away from contaminants.

Method:
Put the flour, yeast, sugar and salt into a bowl and mix with your hands – take your key people to a different environment where they can mix together freely to discuss the vision and mission. Many companies find their people become more creative and engaged away from their usual environment. You'll need to roll up your sleeves and get involved so they mix up and share their ideas.

Stir warm water into the mixture so that it starts to stick together – it can help to have an independent facilitator involved to get people thinking along the same lines and uniting in a common purpose. The mixture might look sloppy at first but as it binds, it will become doughy. Likewise your people may come up with some odd or conflicting ideas about the vision and mission, but they will start to stick together if you keep on mixing them.

Lightly dust a work surface with flour and turn the mixture out onto it. Knead until it no longer feels sticky – once you've got the makings of a vision and mission for your company, change the environment again and really work at it. Knead the draft from every angle – does it work for everyone? Will it stand up to scrutiny? Does it spring back after taking a knock?

Move the dough into a bowl and cover with cling film or put it in a plastic bag. Leave it to prove and double in size – give the vision and mission some shape and then leave it alone for a while. This is a good time to take a break for lunch or do another activity unrelated to work. Don't keep prodding at it while it's proving or you'll ruin it.

Carefully move the dough into a loaf tin, cover with a clean tea towel and leave to prove again. Preheat oven – when taking the vision and mission back to the rest of the company, move it carefully. This is so it doesn't lose its shape when being transported into the hotter, more pressured environment.

Cook until browned and risen – when cooking the vision and mission for the first time, you need to watch it doesn't burn. Sometimes senior managers delegate too soon and think they've left the vision and mission to 'cook' with their team, only to find it's been left too long unattended and has burned.

Leave to stand until cooled before eating – give people a cooling off period to let the vision and mission settle with them so they get used to it.

FOOD FOR THOUGHT...

Where are we going?

When preparing a meal we will need to know what we want to prepare, how we are going to prepare it and when we are going to prepare it. To answer these questions we will need to follow recipes whether written down or carried in our heads. The recipe will have the title of *what* is to be prepared, it will have a list of ingredients and *how* to put them together and finally there will be information about *when* to prepare the dish, how long it will take and other details such as oven temperature, timing and so on.

Running a business is no different. The first thing we have to establish is *what* do we want to achieve, then *how* we are going to achieve it and *when* will it happen. Putting this in business terminology:

- **Vision** is the '*what*' you are going to do;
- **Mission** is the '*how*' you're going to do it.
- And the **goals, objectives** and **targets** are the '*when*' you're going to do it.

Many people confuse terms like:

- Vision
- Mission
- Goals and Objectives

As consultants, we find that many times when we work with a business and ask them what their vision is, we either get a blank look or they start talking to us about goals and objectives or something else.

So at the start of this section let us define our terms. The first one we have to understand is the Vision. The Vision, basically, is the big idea. It is the idea that is going to provide unity and purpose and inspire those around the business. The vision should be uncluttered and easy to understand. It does not necessarily need to say exactly what you are doing but it must give a good idea of where you want your business to go. A business without a vision is like a car with a GPS installed, and the driver not knowing the destination. If you do not know where you are going, you will never make progress, so you must have a clear vision of your destination.

In setting the vision, you need to make sure that all the stakeholders in your business have an understanding of what that vision is. By stakeholders we mean the:

- Owners
- Staff
- Customers
- Shareholders
- Suppliers

These are the ingredients that you need to mix together to create a successful business.

Let us now look at some examples of vision. The first one is NASA. Their vision was *"to put a man on the Moon"*. That is an easy vision to understand although very hard to actually accomplish.

Another famous vision (which has now been superseded) was *"to put a PC on every desk"*. Guess whose vision that was? – If you said Microsoft, you're right.

The interesting thing is that Microsoft does not sell PCs but obviously they need to have a PC on every desk to get their software installed. So in this case the vision is divorced from what they're actually doing, but intimately linked.

Another famous vision is the one that says: *"Quality, service, cleanliness and value";* now despite your own personal views on the actual product sold by this business; that has been McDonald's vision right from the very beginning, when the business was set up by Ray Crock.

The interesting thing about '*to put a man on the Moon*' reminds me of the story of a woman who was working in NASA just prior to putting the man on the moon; John F Kennedy arrived at the NASA Space Centre, saw the woman working there and asked:

"What do you do here?"

And she said:

"I'm helping to put a man on the moon."

NASA managed to get their vision right through the organization, down to operational level. If you can do that in your own business you are most likely going to be a very successful business.

Let us get back to vision. The first thing that vision has to do is provide a clear sense of purpose and direction. It provides motivation for all those around it. It helps coordinate effort and it gives a common frame of reference for all the various stakeholders in the business. The other important thing that vision has got to do is to direct and facilitate change. It is always talking about what *could be* rather than *what is*.

How does this all work in practice? Well, what you have got to do in business is:

- Create the vision
- Set the mission
- Communicate the vision and mission to all of those involved
- Implement the vision and mission

Let us look at an example closer to home.

A soccer team in the Premiership may have a vision that says: **"We want to win the FA Cup."**

So that is the vision. What will be their mission?

The **Mission** will be stated in a way that appeals to each of the various different stakeholders. So the mission is going to make comments about:

"We will need a well coordinated group of athletes who are the best in the country."

The mission will also state that:

"We need to have fans that are going to enjoy the exciting football we're going to play."

The mission may also have some comment about the coaching staff:

"Who will need to be dedicated and skilled to enable the good athletes to achieve their full potential?"

And then the mission is going to talk about some benefit to the owners:

"We will have a nationally recognized team that's going to be a great source of pride and profitability"

The third stage is to communicate the vision and mission; how might this be done with a football team?

So to start with, in business you need to have *a clear vision, a clear mission* and *clear goals and objectives.*

MORE FOOD FOR THOUGHT...

The Rope Analogy

When we do live training sessions we get people to hold a rope up 6 feet high and we ask the audience to tell us: How can people get over the rope?

Now there will be the usual wags who will say:

"Go around it. Lower the rope. Go under it."

But what we are actually asking is: *How do you get over the rope?*

The usual suggestions come up; if you are athletic you could jump over the rope, if you are not you could get a chair and then jump/leap over the rope. You could get someone to give you a leg-up. You might even get a ladder and climb over the rope that way. All these would achieve the objective of getting over the rope at six feet high.

Now, let us put the rope at 100 feet in the air. If we asked the same audience: How will you get over that rope? – They will come up with suggestions like:

"Hire a helicopter to take you over the rope."

Or they might say:

"Get a fire engine ladder and climb it and get over the rope that way."

Some will talk about hiring a crane and going up the crane and getting over the rope. Some people even suggest being fired out of a cannon over the rope.

All these actions achieve getting over the 100 foot rope. And the point is that how you get over a rope six feet high and how you get over a rope 100 feet high are quite different processes.

So you need to start out on your journey using methodologies that are going to get you to your vision (your big idea) and not just take steps that will get you somewhere short of it.

An example we had recently, a woman came to us who wanted to set up a chain of restaurants. When we started talking about it she told us how she had a vision for a chain of restaurants.

So, as part of the consulting process, we were going through all the normal steps she would need to set up the first one. And we were going through what staff to hire, how we would organize menus and so on and so forth. And then we said to her: "We had better set some human resource policies." And she said to us: "Why would I need those? I've only got one restaurant and I only will have about eight or 10 staff."

What she forgot was that her vision was to have a chain of these restaurants and if she is going to build a chain she has to start as she means to go on, because she will need to have robust human resources policies to properly select staff and appoint managers for a chain of restaurants.

Another concept that's important when you are setting your vision is what is called:

The B.H.A.G

It is not our original idea. It comes from an article by James Collins and Jerry Porras called: *Building Your Company's Vision* and later developed in their book **"Built to Last"**

B.H.A.G. stands for:
            B.......................... Big
            H.......................... Hairy
            A.......................... Audacious
            G.......................... Goal

What we are proposing here is that when you set your vision don't set it too timidly, you need to have a **big** vision.

A simple example of this is a client who owns a Deli in south-east London. Her *vision* is to be the food queen of south-east London. It doesn't mention anything about owning a Deli because that is just a part of her mission.

So when you set your vision, set it big because it will become a unifying focal point of effort; and the bigger the vision you have the more effort you are prepared to put in.

A big vision becomes a catalyst for team spirit. It can help the team focus its efforts on what it needs to do to get there. It also provides a clear finish line to know when your **ultimate goal** is achieved.

FIND OUT MORE...

For more tips, tools and resources go to:
www.businesscookerybook.com/resources

Chapter 2

Her vision crystallized at 9.37am on a crisp Monday morning. Jenny was walking Buttons, the family's chocolate Labrador through the park on the way back from school. The timing could have been better. Her 'Eureka!' moment coincided with Buttons' decision to leap through the air into the murky, green pond to chase the squirrel he had spotted on the other side of it.

Usually she would have lost her temper. She knew shouting wasn't the best way to coax him out of the pond, yet she always felt she had to do something to avoid the judging looks from the other dog walkers who pointed to the sign about keeping dogs on a lead near the duck pond. To date, Jenny had never seen a duck on the pond.

As she came to her realization on her vision, she felt elated, "I've been playing far too small."

What triggered her breakthrough was thinking about what she had really enjoyed about being an interior designer. She remembered a project she had worked on when she was the designer-in-residence at the town's department store nine years ago. She was asked to work on the refurbishment of a rather shabby independent hotel which had recently changed hands. The new owners wanted to create a unique environment for their guests which would be a fun weekend retreat for tourists and locals alike.

Over the course of eight months she had worked with them to design and renovate the 12 themed bedrooms and shared spaces. They had been delighted with the result. So were the critics and travel writers, earning the hotel top recommendations in prestigious guide books.

When she started her own interior design business 14 months ago, she'd begun with high hopes, but a few months in found herself settling for much smaller projects. The odd dining room here and nursery there. She didn't feel fulfilled, but reasoned that as a mum working from home it was the best she could hope for. It didn't help that the only referrals she'd received through networking groups were for people looking for a new sofa or choosing wallpaper. They took her advice and then bought the items cheaper on the internet. She learned not to give away any more of her time for free.

Her confidence had definitely taken a knock, however her renewed vision inspired her.

Her mother's words about organizing dinner parties were echoing in her ears. On the phone Barbara had explained to her the need to get the guest list right, "There's no point inviting the wrong people to your party – if you're taking the time to put on the party, don't just settle for 'bums on seats' and invite people to make up the numbers. Also, don't think small and assume that someone's too important to want to come to your party; if you don't ask them, you'll never know. People appreciate being asked, even if they can't make it that time."

"This is exactly what I've been doing," Jenny whispered. "Time to get the right people to the party."

At that moment, she made a pact with herself to focus her attention on those who would help her to achieve her vision of:

"Creating memorable weekends away for 5,000 or more people a year."

Unless her local small business networking groups were going to be filled with hotel owners with thousands of guests each year or could connect her with them, they were a distraction and would delay the realization of her vision.

She pulled out her mobile phone and called Debbie, her virtual assistant. "Debbie, have you got 15 minutes?"

"Sure," said Debbie.

"Great, we need to talk about how we market our services. I've been thinking we should take a new approach."

All by himself, Buttons climbed out of the pond, shook himself off and stood at Jenny's feet with an expectant look on his face that said, "OK boss, time to get going." They started walking as Jenny continued to talk.

By the time they reached the house, Debbie was as excited about the new direction as Jenny was and had come up with a few ideas of her own.

Until Debbie suggested it, it hadn't occurred to Jenny that she could go back to the owner of the hotel she renovated and ask them if she could use their re-fit as a case study. She also realized her website would need an overhaul if she was going to attract the kind of clients she was looking for. Luckily she'd had her site designed on a platform she could edit herself, so that didn't need to hold things up.

She unlocked the front door, Buttons pushed past her into the house and her keys clattered as she tossed them into the bowl in the hall. She went straight to her 'study' taking her jacket off as she walked. Yes, the study was a corner of the sitting room, but calling it her study made it feel like she was going to work in the morning. She rummaged through old drawers and files and finally found what she was looking for. While she was on a roll, she wanted to do something about it. There's no time like the present.

"OK", she said, "deep breath". The butterflies in her stomach were doing back-flips as she held the business card in her hand. She dialed and got straight through to the person she was after. "Good morning Nathan. It's Jenny Richardson. You may remember we worked together on the refurbishment of your hotel a few years ago..."

"Jenny – of course!" Nathan replied. "How are you doing these days?"

Twenty minutes later Jenny was on cloud nine. She'd called to ask if she could photograph the hotel for a case study to put in the portfolio section of her website and she'd been overjoyed to hear how the hotel's popularity had grown after the refit. With an appointment to see the owner next week she couldn't believe she hadn't thought about doing this sooner.

Throughout the journey to work, Simon had been pondering how to get the message across to his directors. He'd noticed since he started that all but one of them had barely spoken to him and appeared to side with the UK Sales Director in every meeting. The decision to appoint him over the Sales Director clearly had not been a popular one, but he was here to improve the profitability of the UK office not make friends, he told himself and buried his feelings.

In his career to date he'd been required to make some tough calls. He knew the world of software publishing was a small one, so it was hardly surprising they had heard about his last role and what he had done. He hadn't wanted to make so many redundancies after the merger, but it just didn't make sense to duplicate roles, especially at the senior levels. The organization was top-heavy and, thinking about what he and Jenny had talked about over the weekend, too many cooks were indeed spoiling the broth.

He didn't blame his new team for being cautious around him. In their position he probably would have felt the same way, especially when their new Managing Director was a former Finance Director with a reputation for cost-cutting. The frustrating part of it was he needed their support. All the time that they were either opposing him in meetings for the sake of it and then behind closed doors nodding and acting like 'yes' men and women to safeguard their jobs, they weren't making progress as a company.

As Simon pulled into his reserved space at the company car park he found the prospect of walking into the building daunting. Knowing the area was covered by CCTV and the receptionist would be watching him sat in his car thinking, he knew it wouldn't look good, so he emerged from his car, grabbed his bag and stood up straight. He strode confidently towards reception. He said Good Morning, signed in and made his way to his office.

There was an hour before he was due to have his morning meeting with his PA Angela, so he closed the door and walked to the window. He'd been stuck in traffic for an hour and knew he thought better standing up, so wondered if this would literally give him a different perspective on things.

He continued his train of thought about the team. The only person who seemed on board was Karen. To say he was surprised would be to put it lightly. She was the HR Director. He hadn't expected her support, given his previous track record. If he'd been a gambler, he'd have put money on her being the person to block his every move.

As it turned out, she didn't seem to play political games and spoke her mind. "Funny how other directors don't invite her to the meetings they chaired", Simon thought as he stared out of the window at nothing in particular. "They say it's because she's part-time, I wonder how true that is."

Whenever he asked her opinion, Karen gave it to him. She clearly relished the opportunity to have an input. He wondered how discrete she would be if he confided in her about his concerns about managing the directors. He usually kept his cards close to his chest. Simon wasn't used to opening up to people he didn't know and he'd only known Karen for a matter of weeks. Even friends he had known since school didn't really 'know' him, Simon thought. He'd had to be guarded about business and personal matters in the past in order to progress in his career, yet he had the nagging feeling that his people skills and leadership skills were about to be tested and that made him feel decidedly uncomfortable.

As his eyes wandered down towards the road outside, his subconscious mind noticed a van stopped at the traffic lights. The catering company's logo caught his eye and his train of thought shifted. He thought back to what he and Jenny had talked about over the weekend. "Am I trying to cook a meal without knowing the recipe?" he asked himself as he mulled over his challenge with the team. "I want to get them on board with a vision for the future, but I'm not even clear about what that vision is and what we're trying to create."

He rationalized this was something outside of his skill-set and there was no shame in not having the skills to do something he hadn't had to do before. "I know that, but admitting I don't have all the answers would be seen as a sign of weakness...wouldn't it?" he thought. Simon could feel the tension building in his body. The familiar knot in his stomach was coming back and as he turned towards the desk and sat down in his leather swivel chair he noticed his hands were clenched into fists.

"There must be a way to get help and still save face." Thoughts raced through his mind, although to anyone peering into the office, he would have seemed calm and reflective. "Maybe I could read a book, and then no one would know. Or I could go on a course. No that wouldn't do. I couldn't sit in a room full of people and risk being put on the spot. How about an audio book? I could listen in the car on the way to work. I learned Italian like that; could it work with managing people?" He started to feel overwhelmed when he realized he didn't even know where to start with choosing something to listen to. "Maybe Karen's got some ideas. She's the expert in people; she might be able to help. But I couldn't ask for help directly..." He had an idea.

He picked up the phone and the sheet of extension numbers. He dialed Karen's number as he knew she came into work early. "Karen, could you come into my office please? I just want to run through some numbers with you."

Ten minutes later Karen appeared laptop in hand ready to go through the hastily prepared budgets and spending for the last 6 months. She looked a little flustered. Simon started off. "Thank you for coming through so quickly. I've been thinking about the managers and directors. I'd like to see whether we can get some sort of course for them so they're all pulling in the same direction. They seem to be all over the place. Do we have any budget to get a trainer or motivational speaker in?"

Karen bit her lip and took a moment to think before replying. She'd wanted to tackle this issue for a couple of weeks now, but from an entirely different direction. She'd been waiting for an opportunity. Now was her chance and she didn't want to mess it up.

"That's a great idea. It would make such a difference having everyone working together," she said. "In my experience these kinds of initiatives go down well and have more of a lasting impact when they come from the top and cascade down. Otherwise, there can be a bit of a 'them and us' attitude going on if the leadership team isn't involved."

"Exactly. That's why I want the directors to go on this course," said Simon.

"Yes, that's true. I've found coordinating everyone's diaries to get them all together for a one-hour meeting can be a nightmare, so getting them all together for a course could be tricky. It sounds like this is something that might be better handled one-to-one. Did you use any executive coaches or mentors at your last company?" asked Karen.

"No, I don't really know much about them. I think one of my colleagues had one to help her work through a personal problem, but I don't see how that would work here," he said.

"It sounds like she might have worked with a counselor or therapist rather than a coach. Executive coaching is different because it's about taking people who are already good at what they do and helping them to be even better. For example," she explained, "take someone who's technically very good at what they do, but they've never needed to learn how to be a leader. They change roles and suddenly find their technical skills aren't as important as the ability to influence others, manage political situations or get them on board with the strategy for the future."

She paused before continuing, "I actually trained as a coach last year and as part of my training, I worked with someone who had been an engineer all his career and then became head of his department. Over a few months he worked on how he managed the very different personalities in his team. He'd been clashing with someone in particular and I helped him to understand how to get the best out of them by adapting his management style."

"This sounds interesting," said Simon. "Could you do something similar here?"

Karen seized on her chance to broach the subject of Simon having coaching but without causing any offence.

"It would create a conflict of interest if I did the coaching, but I've got some good contacts and know experienced executive coaches who could be completely objective and discrete. Of course, if we were going to suggest something to the directors, it would carry more weight if you had a coach as well..."

Simon did his best not to let his sense of relief and excitement show. This gave him the perfect excuse to get support in private and not lose face. "Well, if you think it would help to get the directors' agreement to this, I'd be prepared to have coaching myself. How quickly could we get started?"

"I can make a few calls this afternoon and get some proposals back to you by the end of the week. How does that sound?" she asked.

"Sounds great," said Simon.

As Karen packed up her things and left his office, Simon retained his composure. When she was gone, he walked to the corner of his office, pretended to examine a picture hanging on the wall and almost inaudibly shouted "Yes!" to himself and punched the air beside him.

This was going to be a good week. He couldn't wait to tell Jenny.

Recipe for Defining and Reaching Out to the Target Market, Soliciting Support from Colleagues

Cooking a barbecue often seems a casual affair but in reality requires a lot of planning. Finding out what food will suit the attendees best, preparing it and then delivering it, is very similar to establishing a business. There is no point in cooking something that nobody will eat. Like in business we must provide a product or service people actually want and will value. Too often this is not the case. We need to consult people who may be possible customers for their opinion. Extra hands at a barbecue can be very helpful.

There are also other things that will be required at a barbecue other than the food to make the experience enjoyable. The food may be cooked very well but if we do not have the right plates and utensils the experience may be less than satisfactory.

Putting on a barbecue can also move us out of our comfort zone. Cooking outdoors is an entirely different matter to cooking in our well laid out kitchen with everything at hand.

Ingredients:
Meat, poultry, fish, seafood, various salads, oil, bread or bread rolls, sauces and dressings

Other Requirements:
Barbecue, plates, serving utensils, eating utensils, napkins, foil, skewers

Method:
Prior to the event clean the barbecues and make sure there is enough gas in the bottle – Having worked out who to invite it is important to ensure that we will be properly and have the basic resources to undertake the barbecue. People seeing a dirty barbecue may make them lose their appetite for the food that is going to be produced on it. The initial presentation is key.

Before cooking work out how you are going to lay out the food, utensils, napkins etc. – It is usually better to serve the food cooked on the barbecue first and then have the people put other food on their plate second. This ensures that there is enough room to serve the barbecued food on the plate and that it does not cover other food. In business we have to decide what the most important thing we should focus on is.

Items needing prior preparation should be attended to — it is important to marinate the meat in advance, wrap the fish in foil and put items on skewers.

Allocate tasks – Sometimes the cooking of the barbecue is best delegated to a guest who has the necessary skills. With regard the other food get help to lay it out in a way that ensures a smooth flow for the guests in filling their plates.

Stagger the cooking of the barbecued food so that it can be cooked to meet the various tastes of the attendees– people like their steak cooked to different degrees – rare, medium or well done. It is important to have a range of steaks on the barbecue at once so there is no waiting. Remember not all our clients are the same.

FOOD FOR THOUGHT...

Strategy is not a dirty word

The key thing about strategic planning is you need to ask yourself the question:

"Where will the business go in the next 10 years?"

Or maybe three or five years. The length of the period that you are going to plan for will depend on what sort of business you are in. If you are in a business that does not change very much, is not subject to technology and so on, or a service business, you may be able to plan out for 10 years. If you are in the IT or technology type of business you may find that your planning horizon may be only one year because of constant change and technological advances.

So you will need to decide how long you want to plan for. It may be that you want to exit your business in a certain amount of time, maybe in four years time; if so your planning cycle would be four years.

But we all have different reasons why we are in business and how long we want to stay in a particular business, so when we are deciding the period we want to plan for we first must decide what a useful period to plan for is and is it relevant to plan for that period.

When we are planning we want to make sure that we are building an outline framework of the basic principles and targets that we need to take into account.

In strategic planning there are quite a few things that we might want to look at, for example:

- Our competitive advantage over our competitors
- How we add value to the client – we should always be looking in any plan to see how we can add value.
- Whether to focus on the mass market or a niche market
- The best way to get to that market
- Whether to have cost based strategies
- Whether to compete on low cost structure - something which small and medium-sized enterprises (SMEs) can do well
- Whether to have market based strategies where we go out and find a need and then build a product or service to satisfy that need

Often things do not go exactly to plan and we need to have a Plan B to make sure that when something changes we can immediately adapt our strategy to suit.

We then need to develop and introduce our strategy. And having introduced it we need to make sure that we are continually evaluating it and that we have constant feedback on what is actually happening.

What you have to do in your business first is find a *Competitive Advantage*, if you can.

A second type of strategy is *Cost Advantage* which seeks to answer the question "How can I do things cheaper and still provide a quality service?"

Look at how to lower costs, whatever they are and if you can do this and maintain a lower cost structure than your competitors you may have a cost advantage.

A third type of strategy is *Market Dominance* and even though you might think that small and medium enterprises cannot be market dominant, they can.

You can be market dominant in your local area; for example, one of our clients is a picture framer and what he has managed to do is acquire all the picture framers in his area so now he is dominant in that area in that particular part of his city. He had done this through acquisition.

A fourth type of strategy is: *New Product Development* which finds ways to develop products ahead of rivals.

A fifth strategy might be *Contraction and Expansion* which is based on what we are actually good at, and focusing on that. Quite often our businesses grow willy-nilly because we start doing things because people ask us to do them and we move away from our core competencies.

Maybe there are things in your business that you are doing that are not making an adequate contribution and you should stop doing them and focus on what you are actually good at, which hopefully will be more profitable.

A sixth strategy is *Price Leadership.* This is very hard to do as a small and medium enterprise because it is hard to dominate an industry through price and this type of strategy is not often available to SMEs so we will not labor the point too much. However SMEs with low overheads may be able to create a price advantage over bigger competitors.

One of the strategies you could consider is to *Go Global* where you could expand your business overseas. There are many businesses that can do this, service businesses particularly. But there is still scope for products in many markets as these markets become more affluent. Is this an area you should be looking at?

The eighth strategy is *Re-engineering* where you might look at ways of doing things differently in our business, thinking outside the box or looking at new ways of doing what we do, but in different places and doing it better?

In addition to the market-centered strategies, there are some internal strategies we might put into place. For example, we may *Downsize* by selling off unwanted parts of our business and contract the business to the areas that we know better.

A second internal strategy may be to *De-layer* the business, for example where there is too much bureaucracy; perhaps too many levels of management which would slow down the decision making process. This is an area we may want to look at if we decide to be innovative and to change with the changing environment.

Finally, we could think about: *Restructuring* our business where we should re-think the way our business is organized and do it differently. Maybe different people could work in different parts of the business.

FIND OUT MORE...

For more tips, tools and resources go to:
www.businesscookerybook.com/resources

Chapter 3

The day of the hotel visit came around faster than she thought and as she pulled up outside the building, she could see that things had improved since she was last there.

Derek, the owner, spotted her from the window and came out to the car park to greet her.

"Jenny, how are you? It's been such a long time. Do come in." He enthusiastically held out his hand to shake hers and as their hands met, he clasped his left hand over their grasp.

Derek walked her through the reception area and into his office as they exchanged pleasantries. The staff smiled as she walked through, making her feel welcome. She glanced around each room she passed trying to remember what had changed since she was last there.

"Come in, sit yourself down. Can I get you a cup of tea?" Derek did his best to make Jenny comfortable, she nodded to the tea, "yes please, that would be lovely."

He went outside briefly and returned saying, "tea's on its way."

"So, what's new? The last I remember you were going on maternity leave. Your little one must be about six or seven now." Derek made his way around his large oak desk and sat down.

"He's actually nine and he's growing up fast," she said.

Derek's eyebrows shot up and he leaned back on his chair clasping his hands at the back of his neck, revealing the damp patches on his shirt under his arms. Jenny did her best not to look. He jerked forward and put his arms back down, "How time flies, eh? So just the one?"

"No, no, we have a little girl as well; she's six now." Their tea arrived on a plastic tray.

"You must have your hands full with them, so what brings you back to our little hotel?" he asked.

"Once the kids had started school, I wanted to get back to doing what I loved. Don't get me wrong, I love being with the kids, but I also loved the creativity of design and helping to turn an idea into something really special. So last year I set up on my own and have enjoyed every minute of it." She thought it best not to mention how frustrated she had been with the projects she'd had so far. She was living by the motto, 'fake it til you make it'. Just as the thought crossed her mind, she pushed it away, she already had made it, and she just needed to get back into the swing of things.

"I was going through my portfolio the other day," she added, "and I realized we'd never taken any photos of the hotel. I loved working on the refurbishment so much and I wanted to show other people what was possible. You know how hard it is for people to visualize what can be done with a space? I was even thinking it would make a great case study to put on my website. We could include a link to the hotel's website in case anyone wanted to book a room."

"Well, you know how happy I was with it, so there's no problem in taking photos," he said. "I just hope it's still looking as good as you remember it!"

"That would be fantastic, thank you Derek," Jenny said.

"We've got about an hour before tonight's guests start checking in and I think all the rooms have been made up, so shall we get started?" Derek asked.

"Yes, let's start with the reception area while it's quiet and move on to the themed rooms."

"I've asked housekeeping to keep all the doors open so you can get in and out quickly, so you shouldn't need me with you. Are you OK just wandering around?"

"Sure, it shouldn't take more than 5 minutes in each area," Jenny said.

It's amazing what can be accomplished on a deadline and with just a couple of minutes before the hour was up, Jenny had the shots she wanted. She made her way to Derek's office and found him flicking through some magazines. "All done," she said.

"Let's have a look," said Derek. Jenny held up her digital camera and went through each photo one by one with him, "you've got some good ones there." Derek passed Jenny the magazine he was holding, "what do you think?"

She started flicking through and saw articles about hotels and restaurants across the country, some recipes, days out and lots of classified ads in the back. "Nice magazine," she said unsure what he meant.

He took the magazine back, thumbed his way through until he found what he was searching for, "This - do you think we could do something similar?"

She looked and asked, "An article?"

"Yes. Each month they feature an unusual hotel. I think what we've got here is unusual enough to qualify. There aren't many modern hotels with a Shakespearean theme and a bedroom for each of his plays! Usually if there's anything like it out there it's a bit twee, but you brought it right up to date."

"Hmm," she said, "I hadn't thought of PR, but we could give it a go. I've got no idea how we'd go about it."

"Well, when you find out, let me know!" Derek laughed, but he was deadly serious. This could benefit them both and he hoped Jenny realized that.

"Don't worry, I'll find out," she said.

They both heard the bell at reception. "That'll be our first guests arriving for tonight. I'd better go," said Derek. "It's been great seeing you again." Jenny was about to offer her hand when Derek leaned in and air-kissed her on her right cheek, then the left.

"Thanks Derek," she said. "I've got some lovely shots here. I'll be in touch soon."

Jenny walked back to her car and put her camera on the passenger seat, "PR eh? This could be interesting. Where on earth do I start?"

As the week progressed, Simon found himself wondering what working with a coach would be like and what kinds of people Karen would recommend to him. Should he look for someone who had been in the same position as him or would it be someone who had been a coach their entire career? He really didn't know what look for, but, he reassured himself, it wasn't his job to do that it was Karen's and he was beginning to trust her. It wasn't easy for him to talk to someone about it, but the way she'd handled the issue of getting help, he felt that at the very least she had the company's best interests at heart.

For now he put it to the back of his mind. The weekly update meeting with the directors was about to start. Angela, his PA, popped her head around the door of his office and brought his tea to his desk. "You're a mind-reader, thank you."

"Do you want me to sit in and take notes for this one?" she asked.

"Yes please," he replied.

"OK, I'll start rounding up the troops. I'll start with Andy, he always seems to take the longest to get here and his office is just 50 paces away!" Angela smiled.

Ten minutes later and everyone was sat around the table in Simon's office with one chair noticeably empty. Angela stood up and slipped out of the office. She returned a few minutes later with Andy who strode in, apparently oblivious to the fact he had kept everyone waiting. "Client called and I had to deal with it." He avoided eye contact with Simon.

Simon let it go but was seething inside. He couldn't wait to start working with his coach so he'd know how to handle this in the future.

The meeting went as Simon predicted it would. Andy talked over the top of everyone, complained at the lack of marketing and said that was why sales were down. Then he demanded marketing spend money on exhibiting at trade shows to get his team better leads to work with. Faced with Andy's certainty and not wanting to cause a scene in the meeting, the other directors kept their heads down and went along with him.

Diane, the finance director, eventually pointed out that while sales were down the profitability of the company was falling at a faster rate than sales. She asked whether there were any areas where spending cuts could be made.

Simon could see Andy's face redden. Initially he thought he was embarrassed, but it soon became clear he was angry.

Andy exploded, "I see what's happening here" he exclaimed, directing his comments to Simon and slamming his hands down on the table, "you come in here and you start stripping back. You don't care about the company, the goodwill we have in the market, what we've all worked so hard to achieve. You're about cost-cutting and nothing else. You'll be here a year at most and leave us all to pick up the pieces. This sucks." He shoved his chair back and stormed out of the office leaving everyone stunned.

"Angela," Simon said, "Could you close the door please?" He waited a moment, "OK, next item on the agenda." Everyone dropped their eyes to the agenda and no mention was made of Andy's outburst. Karen was the last to leave after the meeting finished and as she was about to walk through the door Simon called her back for a quick chat about what had happened.

"How are you getting on with finding executive coaches?" he asked.

"I've spoken to a number of them and there are a few who I think would be a good match for you," she said. "I'll get their profiles over to you once I've got some pricing from them."

"That's great. When I get the profiles, how do I choose between them?" Simon asked. "I never judge anyone from their CV alone. I'd rather meet them and hear what they have to say."

"What I'll do then is get a short-list for you and you can have a chat on the phone. If you like the sound of one or two of them, I'll get them in for what's called a 'chemistry meeting'. It's where you can ask them any questions and judge for yourself who you'll feel most comfortable with. How does that sound?" she asked.

"Sounds good," Simon waited before continuing. "What about this business with Andy? Can we get him started with a coach as well?"

"Sure, but I think it would be good if you smoothed things over with him before anyone suggests anything. He might feel he's being picked on if he's the only one having coaching." Simon agreed and promised to talk to Andy. He didn't relish the thought, but he knew he had to act quickly before rumors started spreading around the office.

He walked with Karen to the door and turned to Angela, "Could you ask Andy if he can come and see me please?"

Angela raised her eyebrows and said, "Are you sure?"

"Yes, and don't take no for an answer," he replied. He walked back to his office, sat at his desk and started thinking about what to say when Andy arrived.

Angela thought fast. She'd worked with Andy for three years and had seen him rise through the company. She knew how stubborn he could be if challenged head-on. Usually she'd call his PA, Grace, and ask her to get him to come through, but she also knew how much Grace liked to chatter about any scandals or arguments. Instead she called his direct line, "Andy, have you got a minute? Simon would like a quick chat."

"I'm busy," he grunted. "He'll have to wait."

"I realize that," she said calmly. "Can you spare a few minutes?"

"No, I told you I'm busy," he said.

Angela persisted. "Andy, this would be a great opportunity to talk about what you've been working on with your clients."

"Oh for God's sake Angela, alright. But I can't stay long," he said.

Angela leaned around the door, "He's on his way."

Overhearing the exchange gave Simon what he needed. "So, Andy's working on something with his clients he hasn't told me about", he thought. "Maybe this is our common ground".

As Andy came through the door and made for the chair, Simon put his hand up to stop him. He grabbed his wallet. "Come on, we're going for a coffee" and walked through the door. Andy followed. The walk to the coffee shop was a silent one. It was only two minutes away and yet it felt like an eternity. They ordered, Simon paid and they took two window seats.

"Andy..." Simon said.

"Before you start," said Andy, "we've had enough of cost-cutting. I know you've got a job to do, but we've all been here from the start and we know how to grow this company. Yes, it's a tough time and sales are down, but there's no reason to start laying people off."

"Andy, I've got no plans to lay anyone off," Simon reassured him. "The last few weeks I've been getting up to speed, but we haven't really had a chance to talk about the clients and what we can do for them."

"What do you mean?" he asked.

"Andy, you and your team speak to the clients every day. Listen, I don't pretend to be an expert in the products we sell – that's where I rely on you. You're the expert in our clients. You're closest to the action and you know what's selling and what's not. You know what they're asking for and what they need from us. You get on well with them and talk to them in a way I could never do." Andy was slightly taken aback; he had expected a confrontation.

"Where's all this going Simon?" he asked.

"I've been listening to what's been going on and the meetings we've all been having. You're the only one who ever talks about the clients. As an organization, I'd like everyone to really think about the clients and what we can do for them, rather than developing products in isolation and then wondering why they don't buy or moaning when they have a complaint or technical issue." Andy rocked back on his seat. His body language changed and he looked thoughtful – or was it suspicious? He took a risk.

"I agree," Andy sat forward with his hands open and looked animated, "OK, here's what I've been thinking. I've been talking to our key accounts and something they're all asking for is more help understanding the full functionality of what we do. I reckon they're only using about 25% of it so they aren't getting the results they should. We've got an online support ticket system and a premium-rate help line, but they don't like using them. My team's tried to sell in-house training courses, but they all say their budgets have been cut and in a lot of cases there are only a handful of users so it works out too expensive per head."

Simon signaled for him to continue as he sipped his coffee. Andy carried on talking, "Well, I've asked a few clients what they'd like instead and they said they'd be interested in open training courses they could send their staff on. They also said it would be useful for their staff to hear how other people are using the software outside of their own company." Simon nodded for a few moments and allowed what he had just heard to sink in. Andy took the opportunity to knock back his espresso now it had cooled.

Eventually Simon spoke, "That could work. In fact we could probably generate more revenue from one open course than we would by running a few in-house courses."

"You know what?" said Andy smiling, "for once I wasn't thinking about the targets. I was thinking how we could get our clients using the software properly and get some really good case studies and referrals."

"Which would lead to more clients, more users and more revenue," Simon pointed out.

"Exactly," said Andy.

"I like it. Would you put together a proposal for next week's meeting and we'll talk through how we could make this work?" suggested Simon.

Andy smiled and nodded, "Look, about earlier. I was out of line and I shouldn't have said that."

"Enough said."

They both looked at each other expectantly. Andy broke the silence, "I'll talk to Diane when we get back. What I said wasn't directed at her, but she might have taken it that way."

"OK, sounds like a good call. I'm sure she'll be fine," said Simon.

They cleared away their cups and made their way back to the office. As they came through the doors into the open-plan office, Simon instinctively put his hand on Andy's back. It felt like the natural thing to do and neither of them gave it any thought. The staff watching out of the corners of their eyes did and it sent out a big signal - things had been sorted out.

Recipe for Market Research and Customer Value Proposition

It is imperative that we do an appropriate amount of detailed market research to establish if there is a need for our product or service. Such market research must also be on going to ensure that we become aware of any changes in the customer's needs. We also need to understand their needs so that we can position our customer value proposition accordingly. What value the customer sees in our product will have a considerable impact on the price we can charge.

If we were preparing a buffet we would need to know who our customers are going to be and what will their likely price point be. An advantage of buffets compared to table service is that diners have a great deal of choice and the ability to closely inspect food before selecting it. Likewise in today's world of the internet and social media our customers are much more knowledgeable and they often inspect our product or service long before we know they are in a 'buying state'.

Ingredients:
A range of appetizers, entrees, salads, hot dishes, cold dishes, drinks

Method:
Find out the type of customers that may be availing themselves of the buffet– Make sure you know who is going to eat from the buffet and what the alternatives are like *à la carte* service. There are benefits of a buffet because of the wide choice it offers, however not everyone will want that benefit. Some may prefer the more personalized table service. Does our Customer Value Proposition (CVP) suit both or are we only targeting one of the groups.

Based on time of the year work out what might be the right mix of dishes to provide taking into account seasonality of ingredients and special needs of customers – the needs of our customers vary depending on a range of factors. In recession "value for money" may be the mantra. In better times how customers perceive value may change. Remember not all the customers are the same so our CVP needs to appeal to all the customers in our market segment.

Set up tables for buffet in such a way that allows for food to be put in the correct order and allow for ample room for people to move around – we need to ensure that it is easy for customers to do business with us. Slow moving lines at a badly laid out buffet can give the wrong impression even if the food quality is excellent.

Make sure staff are positioned correctly where certain dishes need to be personally served to clients– at certain buffets like a breakfast or carvery, certain foods have to be served to the customers by staff. At a breakfast buffet there is no point in having the egg or omelet cooking person at the end of the buffet. Orders for these should be taken first before the customer moves along selecting the rest of their food. The egg or other item can then be served to them just before they leave the buffet to go to their table.

FOOD FOR THOUGHT...

How do we stand out from the crowd?

We need you to answer the question: *"Why should customers deal with us?"* which means we need a **Customer Value Proposition**

And the answers are <u>not</u> things like:
- We give good customer service
- We go the extra mile

Because we are sure all your competitors say the same thing.

We want you to really think about what is <u>unique about the way you do business</u>. You need to know what differentiates you from your competitors because it is these things that are going to be important in helping you grow your business.

What we want you to do is think of three to five things that are unique about your business. You will find this very difficult, but you need to really try and uncover things that are unique to you, things that you are doing now or that can be made unique for you in the future.

Two examples of how small things can make big differences

Patrick White would like to tell you a story here about how you can have a small competitive advantage which can have a significant difference:

"My first business as an entrepreneur was a motel. I moved into a town in a tourist area where there were lots of motels.

"After examining the market I found that most of them were basically charging the same room rate which meant from the customers' point of view that there was not much differentiation between the motels. This did not seem to be a good way to operate my business so I had to look around to find some way to get a competitive advantage.

The first thing that I noticed was that in motel directories the most expensive hotels are listed first – 5 star, 4 star, 3 star, 2 star and "bring your own tent" type of hotels. My first object was how to get listed first, which meant I had to put the price up, to put me in a different price bracket to the rest of the motels in town.

You cannot just put your price up without giving some value so I had to look around and find some way to give value. In the end the solution was quite simple.

In Australia and New Zealand when you go to a motel they provide a jug, sugar and tea and coffee and usually those small bottles of UHT milk or creamer. This goes against the usual grain for people from down-under because milk is usually in plentiful supply and it's not that expensive. So one of the things I decided to do to give myself a competitive advantage when people came to my motel was that I would give them fresh milk and when they checked in I would, as part of the check-in process, tell them that I would be taking fresh milk when I show them to the room.

That was another thing we did differently. Instead of just giving people the key and telling them where to go and letting them struggle up and down stairs with their bags and children, we used to take them to the room, jug of fresh milk in hand and when I got to the room I would open the door, put the fresh milk in the fridge and then check the room was fine.

You wouldn't believe it, the fact that we provided fresh milk became a major competitive advantage.

Many of our customers told their friends that: "If you go and stay at this motel they not only take you to the room, they also give you fresh milk."

So we ended up with a competitive advantage of providing fresh milk.

For 20 cents extra expenditure we got a $20 premium on the room rate. How simple is that?

Another example of competitive advantage is when I owned a restaurant. One of the things I observed, having owned the restaurant for a short time, is that many people either forget their glasses or because of vanity do not like to wear their glasses when they go out.

Restaurants usually have dim lighting so it can make it hard to read the menu; and I asked myself "How could I create a competitive advantage out of that?"

I thought about it for a little while and then went down to the local chemist. I bought several pairs of those cheap $2 glasses that have different strengths for vision.

So when we say people struggling with reading the menu we would go out with a tray of glasses and say to them: "Do you know what eyesight strength you need?" and we would give them the glasses so that they could read the menu.

This became quite a joke and also became quite a competitive advantage because these customers would go around telling everyone: "When you go to this restaurant, they think of everything. If you can't read the menu they'll even bring out glasses for you."

FIND OUT MORE...

For more tips, tools and resources go to:
www.businesscookerybook.com/resources

Chapter 4

Jenny dialed and heard the familiar international ringtone, the call was answered, "Hola."

"Mum, it's me," said Jenny.

"Hello love," said Barbara. "You don't normally call during the day; is something wrong?"

"No, everything's fine. In fact it's better than fine!" Jenny said excitedly.

"Oh yes....? What's going on? I am going to be a grandmother again?" Barbara asked.

Jenny could hear Barbara whispering "It's Jenny" to her father. She could picture her waving frantically to get his attention in case there was a big announcement.

"No Mum, nothing like that! I wanted to let you know about something I've been working on since we last spoke," she said.

"What's that love?" asked Barbara.

"Well, when we were talking about the dinner party..." said Jenny.

"Did it go well?" asked Barbara.

"What?" Jenny was confused.

"The dinner party," Barbara said.

"I decided to cancel it and go for drinks instead. Mum, listen, I thought about what you said and realized I could follow the same formula in my business. A recipe for success, I suppose. I did what you said and thought about the kind of 'dinner party' I wanted, who I wanted there and I decided to focus on hotel refurbishments."

"That's a good idea," said Barbara. "Didn't you do one of those when you were working at the department store?"

"Yes, well remembered!" Jenny said. "I got in touch with the owner of the hotel last week and I've just been round there to take some photos for my portfolio and he suggested approaching some of the magazines for the hospitality industry and trying to get an article in there. I've never done anything like it and I don't really know where to start. I'd like to do it. What do I do? Write a press release or something?"

"You could," said Barbara, "but it would probably go in a pile of press releases. If it's blatantly selling you or the hotel, they'll just pass it to the advertising sales team and they'll try and sell you an advert. Do you know anyone on the magazine you want to pitch to?"

"No, not at all. It's not my world and I've only just decided to work with hotels so I don't have any contacts. This is more your world Mum. Things can't have changed much since you sold the agency."

"Most of my contacts have moved on," said Barbara, "but there's nothing like picking up the phone and pitching the story. With the internet and email everyone got lazy and started bombarding journalists with irrelevant pieces. If I were you, I'd take a couple of hours and write out a plan before doing anything. It'll help your story to really stand out."

"Mum, I haven't got time to write a business plan, I've only got a few hours a day I can work," Jenny insisted.

"You know that saying 'if you fail to plan, you plan to fail'?" said Barbara. "It's very true. You need to be really clear about how this is going to fit in with how you'll grow your business, the kinds of leads you're interested in and how you'll follow up with the leads the article would generate. It's going to have a bearing on how you pitch the article and which magazines, papers and websites you pitch it to. A plan doesn't have to be a huge document; you can work with one piece of paper if you've got the right information on there. Think of it like the dinner party or just cooking a meal. You need to know what you're making before you start or you won't have all the ingredients to hand. You also need to know which saucepans and utensils you need, which temperature to heat the oven to and so on. A plan keeps you focused. It sets out who you're trying to reach, why they should listen to you and what you're trying to say. You also need to be clear about your 'call to action'."

"What's a 'call to action'?" Jenny felt very ignorant about the world of marketing and PR.

"It's where you tell someone what to do to take the next step," explained Barbara. "You can't just hope they know what to do. If you want them to phone you, tell them the number and tell them to phone you. If you want them to go to your website to download something tell them where to go. What's the call to action for this article?"

"Hire me?" Jenny said with a hint of sarcasm.

"That might be a bit too direct, but I'm sure you can say something that will get them contacting you. You could also think about running a small advert in the magazine so you can share all your details in case the magazine won't publish your number or website." She could hear her mother's hand go over the mouthpiece, muffling a brief conversation, "Jenny, your father's telling me we need to head out to the market before all the fresh fruit goes. I'd love to stay and chat, but I do need to go, we're giving my friend Sally a lift into town and she'll be waiting."

"It's okay Mum, I think I can take it from here," she said.

Jenny looked at her watch – 1:41pm. "I've got about an hour before I need to head off to get the kids," she thought. "Maybe I could get Debbie started on this."

She picked up the phone and dialed her number from memory, "Debbie, hi how's it going?"

"Good thanks," said Debbie. "What's up?"

Jenny explained what had happened at the hotel and her subsequent discussion with her mum.

Debbie replied, "It's not something I've got a lot of experience of, but I could look and see whether there's any information on the internet on how to do it and send it over to you. What do you think?"

"That'd be great - then I can have a look later when the kids are in bed." said Jenny.

Later that evening, Jenny opened her email inbox to find 23 new messages. About half were from Debbie with links to articles and the rest were from people she didn't know sending her information about how to do PR, social media, article-writing, blogging and getting on the radio. "Debbie must have signed me up for their information," she thought. She only got through a few of them when she felt the tension rising in her and her throat and chest tighten. She rested her chin on her left palm as her right hand controlled the mouse. Jenny looked serious and was slumped over the desk.

Simon looked up from the TV when the commercial break started, "Everything OK?" She didn't hear him. He rose and stood behind her. She still didn't notice him so he gave her a quick kiss on the neck. Jenny jumped and laughed. He spun her chair around so she was facing him. "What are you working on?"

"Oh," she shrugged and let out a sigh, "I don't even know. That hotel wants me to get some publicity for the work I did."

"That's great news," Simon said."

"It would be if I had any idea how to do it. Debbie said she'd send me over some information but I've haven't got a clue where to start. It's completely overwhelming. All of these people seem to tell you different things. How on earth do you make a decision on what to do?"

"Why don't you ask your Mum?" asked Simon. "She used to do this sort of thing all the time, didn't she?"

"I did and she gave me some good ideas. I guess I wanted to do this for myself and not go running to her all the time for advice," Jenny admitted.

"You can be so stubborn sometimes," he smiled and gently stroked her face. "Why do you always make it so hard for yourself? You'll learn how to do it if you let your Mum show you. She's got her head screwed on right, you know?"

"I suppose," Jenny was still reluctant. "I wanted my business to be *my* success though. It won't feel like that if someone else has made it successful. It would feel like cheating."

"Jenny now you're being arrogant," he could see she didn't like what he'd just said. "You remember how you talked to your Mum about dinner parties?" she nodded. "If you were cooking a meal you'd never made before, you wouldn't expect to guess at the ingredients and how to make it and then get it right first time. There's a recipe for getting PR and your Mum knows it. Get her to teach it to you, and then you can go out and make it happen. It'll still be your success."

"You're right," said Jenny. "I've got to swallow my silly pride – hey, there's another food reference!" They both laughed.

"So you'll talk to your Mum again?" Simon smiled at her.

"Yes, tomorrow," Jenny agreed.

~

Simon looked at the profiles on his desk. Karen had given him a small folder with information three executive coaches she had short listed for him to speak to. They seemed quite different and the photos were helpful.

He closed the file and thought, "Whenever I've hired people I've always judged them on what they say, not how they look on paper." He pulled out the sheet of paper where Karen had given all of their contact details and started at the top of the list with a coach called Sasha.

Her office number was answered promptly and politely. The receptionist explained that Sasha was currently with a client, but would be finished in 40 minutes time. Simon left his name and number and moved onto the next name on the list, Toby. There was only a mobile phone number which went to voicemail so Simon left a message with his contact details.

Finally, he called Michael and got straight through to him. They chatted for 25 minutes about Michael's coaching qualifications and where he trained. Michael was keen to name-drop large companies he had worked for as a Director, which business leaders he had met and his role on the board of a charity. When Simon mentioned some of the areas he'd like help with, it led to a story about how Michael had been in a similar situation and how wonderfully he had dealt with it.

"If I can't get a word in edgeways on the phone," Simon thought, "what's it going to be like working with him as my coach?" Eventually Simon made excuses about another meeting starting soon, explained that he had a few coaches to talk to and Karen would be in touch.

"Phew," he thought as he hung up the phone, "I'll let Karen handle that one."

He began to check his emails and the phone rang with the ringtone indicating it was his direct line. Simon answered and it was Sasha returning his call. She sounded friendly and efficient; she explained Karen had given her a short brief but she wanted to hear directly from him the areas he would like to work on. There was something about her manner that made Simon feel at ease talking about his current situation.

It was clear from the questions she asked that she'd coached people in his position before and he felt in safe hands. "I'm going to ask you a question that might seem a little direct," she said, "but what are you looking for from a coaching program?" He wasn't quite sure how to respond, so she continued. "What will you be able to do differently as a result of us working together?"

He thought about it.

She sensed he was thinking, so gave him as much time as he needed, which as it turned out was only about 30 seconds – a period of time which always seems longer than it is when you're trying to come up with the answer to a question.

"I've been tasked with improving the profitability of the company. I'd like to be able to get everyone working towards achieving that," he said.

"That's great Simon," said Sasha. "Just so I'm clear, apart from the financials, how will you know that's happening - so I know what we need to work towards?"

"Good question. I suppose people will be coming to me with ideas and suggestions they've really thought through. When I hear the directors talking to each other, it'll be about how they can work together rather than arguing," Simon said. "The meetings will be more harmonious."

"What about you? How will you feel?" asked Sasha.

"I'll feel in charge, respected and trusted." He paused and his voice softened, "I just don't feel that right now." Sasha gave him a moment to compose himself. Simon continued, "You know, it's so good just to talk this through. It's the first time I've ever said anything like that to anyone, even my wife."

"Believe me, you're not alone," said Sasha. "I work with a lot of senior people and you'd be amazed how many of them feel the same way when we start working together. When they say 'it's lonely at the top', they're not kidding, are they?" Simon could hear the smile in her voice and knew he'd found his coach.

"So, Sasha, this is something we can work on?" asked Simon.

"Absolutely. From what you've told me, it sounds like we need to position the message about improving profitability so that it really resonates with the senior team. Once you've got the message right and they understand their part in achieving it, we can move on to the people skills. You've got a bit of work to do to gain their trust and I'll tell you what you can do and how to do it. This falls slightly outside the boundaries of what would be the text book definition of coaching, but I think given the time frame we need to work in, we'll do some mentoring and even one-to-one training to get you to the point where you're getting the results you want. Is that OK with you?" Sasha asked.

"Sounds good," he said. "What happens next?"

"If you're happy for us to work together, let Karen know and I'll arrange all the paperwork with her. How soon did you want to get started?" she asked.

"As soon as possible?" Simon was keen to begin.

As they made the arrangements and said goodbye, Simon felt lighter and more clear-headed than he had for weeks.

He realized he was humming to himself when Angela knocked on his door clutching a piece of paper, "Someone called Toby rang when you were on the phone. He said he was returning your call." She passed him the number and left.

Simon knew his mind was already made up, so called Karen's extension and explained. She would sort out the details with Sasha and explain to the other coaches he had chosen someone else.

The next week Simon's first meeting with Sasha went well. He was amazed how much they could cover in two hours. He also appreciated her input and how much she challenged him on exactly what he meant when he explained his strategy for improving the profitability. "No wonder I've struggled to get people's support," he thought when he considered how hard he had found to explain it to her without slipping into 'finance-speak' as she put it, "I've been talking a completely different language."

She helped him to clarify the short-term and medium-term goals, set out the targets for each quarter and what this would mean to the average member of staff. This was harder than he expected.

He knew it was a sales-driven company, so had expected the staff to be focused on the numbers; he hadn't considered they might be motivated by anything else. It made him confident and at the same time he doubted himself when he realized how much he still had to learn about leadership.

As Sasha explained to him - in order to lead, you need to have followers. People will only follow something or someone they believe in. Money is actually way down most people's priorities. Assuming they are on an appropriate salary for what they do, feeling valued, listened to and that what they do has meaning are all much further up the list.

Recipe for Business Planning & Budgeting

Cooking Japanese food requires a lot of planning. Different combinations of ingredients give rise to a variety of sushi foods. For example with the recipe for California Roll sushi we can get different results from the same resources depending if we want classic sushi or inside out rolls. It will depend whether the nori (seaweed) is on the bottom of the rice or on top of the rice and how we roll it. Business is the same. We will have a variety of resources available to us (people, equipment, money etc.) but the results we achieve will depend on how we mix those resources together.

It is important therefore that we look at all the outcomes we could achieve and select the one that will make the best use of the resources we have. It maybe we need to change one resource for another. In the recipe below we have used imitation crab sticks instead of real crab. This makes it easier to make, cheaper to buy and some would say tastier. Maybe we could replace direct mail marketing with self generated PR.

Ingredients:
Sushi rice, nori sheets, imitation crab sticks (Surimi), avocado, cucumber, sesame seeds

Method:
Take half a nori sheet and cover with rice – 1cm high – make sure our plans have some flexibility to meet the circumstances we may encounter. When we handle the nori we need to make sure our hands are as dry as can be. However for the rice we need to keep them wet to overcome the stickiness of it. In business our plans need to be adaptable to different circumstances.

Flip the nori so that the rice is facing down and start placing the filing for the Californian role – Here we are making a commitment to creating the roll with the rice on the outside. In our business we have to weigh up all the options but eventually we have to decide on which strategy to follow and plan accordingly.

Line up the crab sticks: in pairs or singles – depends how thick you want the role to be – the crab sticks are the main taste influencer in the California roll. In our business we need to know what the main drivers (influencers) are and how they affect the decisions we need to make. If we were substitute smoked salmon for the crab the taste of the roll would be quite different. Similarly if one of our business drivers changes we may need to make different decisions.

Business Cookery

Next to it, line up a 2-3 cucumber sticks – the taste here is not as exciting as the crab but provides a firmness and stiffness to the rolls. If we are planning for growth we need to ensure all our back-office functions are in place to give us stability.

On top of both crab and cucumber sticks, put a large slice of avocado – be careful of any assumptions you make in your plan or budget. Another name for avocado is alligator pear because of its rough exterior skin. We may assume the interior is the same as the exterior and miss out on the opportunity to savor its marvelous taste and texture.

Make sure all ingredients are equal in size and proportion, and roll. Sprinkle outside with some sesame seeds for decoration – using our resources in the right mixture is paramount to our success. The right mix of cash resources, talented people, culture and technology will have a significant impact on the outcomes we achieve.

FOOD FOR THOUGHT...

Understanding the Numbers

Everybody in a business does better when they understand how financial success is measured and how they have an impact on the business's performance. This is *Financial Intelligence* (FI). It helps people feel more involved and committed.

All of us that work in the business are in business and hence we need to speak the language of business. We need to be business people who do business.

To have Financial Intelligence we need for distinct skills:

1. We need to understand the foundation of FI i.e. how to read a Balance Sheet, Profit and Loss and Cash Flow Statement.
2. We need to understand the art behind creating the numbers – finance and accounting are an art as well as a science. We need to understand the assumptions made by the accountants. We need to be prepared to question and challenge the numbers.
3. We need to understand an analysis of the numbers. This requires us to be familiar with ratios and investment analysis, return on investment and so on. Analysis helps you make better decisions.
4. We need to understand the big picture as numbers cannot tell us the whole story. The business's financial results must always be understood in context, within the framework of the big picture.

Experience tells us that many people from non-financial backgrounds are often weak in this area and hence put themselves at a disadvantage. This means they cannot speak the language of finance, know what questions to ask or how to connect the dots between financial results and their inputs.

Tick off how many of the following essential questions you can answer:

- What is our break-even point?
- What are our fixed costs per unit/hour?
- What are our variable costs per unit/hour?
- What is our marginal revenue/cost per unit/hour?
- What are the opportunity costs of what we are doing?
- At what point do diminishing returns set in?
- What is our price elasticity of demand?

An inability to answer any of these questions could be fatal for your business.

FIND OUT MORE...

For more tips, tools and resources go to:
www.businesscookerybook.com/resources

Chapter 5

The timing could not have been better. Jenny took her mum's advice and started reading the online magazines and blogs for the hospitality industry. She didn't really like reading things on her computer. She much preferred to hold a magazine in her hands and flick through the pages but since her local newsagent didn't stock many trade magazines this was the next best thing. Jenny found herself skimming the articles catching the gist of what they were saying: the market was more competitive because people could compare prices on the internet, the rise of the 'staycation' where more UK residents were staying within the country, the need to provide extra, chargeable services to improve profitability and so on.

When she was beginning to tire, she spotted an advertisement for an exhibition for hoteliers and restaurateurs. The fact there would be free seminars appealed to her and she realized this would be a good opportunity to find out what was going on in the market – plus she'd be able to talk to people and possibly network. She could drop the kids off at school and head into the city then still be back in time to collect them.

The decision was made. Within minutes her ticket was booked and the printer whirred into action to produce a copy of her confirmation.

A couple of days later she pulled into the car park at the exhibition centre and grabbed her confirmation from where it lay on the passenger seat. It had been quite a while since she'd been to anything like this and she couldn't quite decide if the butterflies she felt were excitement or dread. "Excitement", she said aloud and she repeated it silently in her head as she collected her badge at the registration desk and picked up a copy of the seminar schedule.

The exhibition hall was filled with all manner of companies from online travel companies and wedding planners through to florists and tablecloth suppliers.

"There are a few companies here I could use," she thought and she started filling her plastic bag with brochures, price lists and business cards.

An announcement went out over the PA system to say that the seminars were about to start. She checked the schedule again and decided the talk on 'Standing out from the crowd' from a marketing agency would be a good place to start. "I might learn something myself here!"

Before the talk started, she got chatting to the person next to her, who was the duty manager for a busy hotel in the city, attending before his shift started later that afternoon. Her curiosity got the better of her and once they had struck up a friendly conversation she had to ask, "If your hotel needed to be refurbished who would be the person making the decision on design?"

He shifted in his chair. She sensed her question had made him uncomfortable, so reassured him she was just trying to understand how the process usually works. He relaxed, "Well I suppose the General Manager together with the owners. We had a refurbishment about two years ago and if I remember rightly the General Manager had a lot of meetings with the architects about the interior. I think they had their own designer." He smiled as he remembered helping the young woman carry the sample books into the General Manager's office and the way their eyes met. He stared into the distance as his mind wandered, "...yes, they did have a designer."

Their conversation was cut short and the speaker took to the stage. Forty minutes later she finally understood the expression Simon used a lot, 'Death by PowerPoint'. She'd expected more from the seminar. Perhaps something she could take away and use in her business. Not the constant switching from case study to pitch to case study to pitch to quotes from happy clients and a request for everybody's business cards. Although she didn't get much from the talk, she did get an idea about how to target hotels from the duty manager she spoke to. She'd been thinking she would need to contact all the hotels and hope that someone was thinking about a refit. The thought filled her with dread. All the rejections from people saying, "Sorry we don't have any plans to refurbish" or "you've missed out – we've just finished". Jenny shuddered. That wasn't her idea of fun.

The thought of working hand in hand with architects felt like a much more natural way of working. This she could do.

She took the show guide out of her bag and scanned the pages with new eyes. Suddenly she noticed the exhibitors who had been invisible to her previously – two firms of architects.

Quickly she collected her belongings and set off into the exhibition hall. After wandering and gathering her bearings, she found the first stand. There was the customary business card bowl to enter a draw, so she dropped a card in slightly embarrassed that she was still using the cards she'd had printed when she started her business. The card didn't reflect her new direction, but as she told herself it didn't really matter, it was just a draw.

The smart-looking man welcomed her and asked about her day so far, trying to establish if she was a possible client for the firm. As soon as he found out what she did, his manner changed and he seemed keen to conclude the conversation. When he was no longer making eye contact with her and looking past her, scanning for other people to talk to, she decided it was time to move on.

"How rude," she thought to herself. Her feelings of anger soon developed into rejection as she walked away, "maybe it was something I said. Maybe he could tell I was small and working from home. I'm not sure I'm cut out for this," she sighed. "Come on, you can do this," another voice inside her started taking over. "You can do this. Just find the other stand and talk to them. Don't try and sell, just talk. Find out how things work." She stood up straight, took a deep breath and set off down the aisle to the other firm of architects.

Jenny started browsing the brochures and leaflets on the stand; the exhibitors were all busy talking to other visitors and that was okay because she enjoyed eavesdropping and was interested to hear what they said to people.

She got a completely different vibe about these people. They seemed friendly, knowledgeable and above all had a passion for good design. There was laughter on this stand where it had been lacking at the other. "Hello there, are you having a good day today?" she caught a glimpse of the name badge which read Tony.

"Yes thanks, you?" she replied.

"I love these events. I love connecting with our clients and finding out what's going on for people. Are you in the hospitality business?" he asked.

"In a way. I'm just getting back into the swing of things after taking a few years out, so it's nice to hear what's going on." Tony looked curious so she continued. "I've been an interior designer and project manager for about 13 years and had a break for my kids. My last big project was a hotel refurbishment, which was so rewarding and the hotel owner's still reaping the rewards."

They continued talking and she could almost see the cogs whirring in Tony's mind. "Do you have a card?" he said.

She felt herself blush as she went to her bag to get a card out. The design on the card was good, yet the photos on the back showed children's bedrooms and living rooms. She felt the need to explain, "I also do a small amount of residential work, this is the card I use at small business networking events." The explanation seemed to satisfy him and he handed out a card of his own.

As Jenny walked away after the conversation had come to a natural end, she didn't notice Tony talk to his pregnant colleague and say, "This lady looks interesting. How long is it before your maternity leave starts?"

"Three months," she replied.

"Hmm...I might get her to come in." He opened his jacket and put Jenny's card in his inside pocket.

~

"Ready?" Andy said clutching his laptop bag and coat in his arm. Simon closed his emails down and confirmed he was ready to go. "We've got about an hour to get there and the traffic's not too bad at this time of day," Andy talked as they walked to the car park together.

In the car Andy chose not to turn the radio on but to use the time to discuss the meeting ahead plus his plans for taking the training courses forward, assuming they had a positive outcome from this meeting. They talked about the personalities of the people they were meeting and how they would handle the meeting.

Andy had put together a folder for Simon to look through in the car with the sales so far this year and where he thought they could add value to clients. He had prepared a presentation about the training courses which would be delivered at a later date. It looked impressive. For the time being this was a 'meet and greet' to find out about the clients' thoughts on the courses.

Simon had no idea so much preparation went into sales meetings. He felt guilty about his preconceived ideas about 'salespeople' and how he'd dismissed them in the past as just being good talkers, even a little bit slimy.

On their return journey, Simon swallowed his pride and asked Andy more about how he knew how to handle such different personalities. The two people they had just met seemed like chalk and cheese, yet Andy got on well with both of them. Simon would have naturally talked more to the detail-orientated manager and ignored the manager who he deemed 'fluffy'.

"About 18 months ago, I went on an NLP course – Neuro-Linguistic Programming," Andy replied. "It helped me to understand what motivates different people, how to pick up on subtle signals and how to establish rapport quickly. I suppose the most important skill I learned was to stop talking and really listen to what the person in front of me is saying. Believe me, that was hard! All my sales training before then had focused on having a pitch prepared, knowing how to handle objections and closing the deal. These were all essential skills, but the missing piece was active listening." Simon looked curious. "Active listening," Andy explained, "is where you are actively paying attention to what's being said and also what's not being said. It's different from hearing, which is a passive activity. You know how sometimes when someone's talking you switch off and only focus on when you can say what you want to say? I don't mean you personally, I mean people in general." Simon nodded. "When you're actively listening you can't have all of that going on in the background or you miss things. You have to pay close attention. It's also about being comfortable with pauses and silences in the conversation. When you take a moment before responding, you find people tell you all sorts of things once they've had a chance to think."

Simon had a flash-back to his coaching session with Sasha and realized that she'd been actively listening and using pauses to help him think and open up. He had experienced firsthand what it was like to have someone truly listen without interrupting, and he enjoyed it. "I think I know what you mean," said Simon. "So is this how you worked out the clients would be interested in open training courses?"

"Yes," said Andy, "and based on the meeting we've just had, I think they'll go for it. We'd need to get a few more companies on board, but I think we can safely say when we launch the courses they'll send at least three of their staff along."

Later that afternoon, all the directors met for the team meeting. Simon asked Andy to present the work he had done so far on developing the courses. The reception was very positive and Simon wondered whether he had been the last person to know about this project since everyone had come with fully-formed ideas on how to make it work. No matter, the good thing was they were all behind the plans.

The next step was to work on the marketing of the courses. This is where Rebekah the Marketing Manager's skills were called for. She had been with the company for about six months and the feedback Simon had received about her was that operationally she was great but didn't come up with many ideas. Simon reserved judgment. He knew the decision to hire a Marketing Manager had been a controversial one and her reporting line hadn't been very clear from the outset, even he wasn't too sure how she fitted in. Perhaps with a new challenge she could add value.

He didn't want to go over Andy's head by calling her in without him, equally she didn't report to Andy and there had been some friction in the past over an advertising campaign. He wasn't sure what to do. What would Sasha suggest? He dialed her direct number and got straight through to her. "Sasha, do you have a couple of minutes?"

"I've got a session with a client in about half an hour, but I can talk for about five minutes before I need to get ready," she said.

Simon explained the situation and asked her advice. "Simon, you know more about this situation than I do. If you were listening to someone else tell you what you've just told me, what would you advise?"

It was the shift in perspective he needed. "Thanks Sasha, that helps. I'm going to speak to Andy, it's his project."

The next number he dialed was Andy's, "Andy, great meeting. Well done, they seemed to like the idea."

"Thanks Simon."

"Now we just need to get the marketing organized for it. Rebekah looks after that, doesn't she? How much does she know about the project already?"

"I'm not sure," replied Andy. "She's probably heard about it by now."

Alarm bells were ringing in Simon's head. This project would be unlikely to succeed if no one knew about it! The salespeople could speak to their clients, but they had their targets to meet and couldn't spend all their time selling courses. Andy sensed that he might have overlooked speaking to Rebekah and tried to cover himself by saying, "Strictly speaking she reports to you Simon."

"That may be true. Andy, we do need to work as a team and Rebekah's part of the team. Can I rely on you to keep her up to date with what's going on? I'll speak to her about what we need."

"Sure," agreed Andy.

The conversation ended more abruptly than Simon would normally have liked, especially as they had had such a good morning with the client. At the same time, he couldn't have Andy leaving people out of the planning process. It seemed odd that everyone else in the earlier meeting knew about the project and was on board, yet the person who would be responsible for spreading the word about it was uninformed.

The next day Simon decided to find out more about the strained relationship between sales and marketing. It was one of the days Karen the HR Director worked, so he took the opportunity to ask her when she came to his office. "Karen, I'm a bit confused about the reporting structure for Rebekah in marketing."

"Ah," said Karen. "This is something that's been going on for a while. She was hired by your predecessor just before he left. I feel sorry for her, she's kind of been left floating and people have passed the buck. She's been doing her best, but she needs direction. At the moment she's playing safe and keeping her head down. It's a shame really because she's bright and has some very good ideas, but she's also quite shy so she never tells people about them!"

"I see," Simon was thoughtful. He continued, "Marketing is going to become even more important in this company in the coming months. We can't afford to let talent go to waste. What do you suggest Karen?"

"I do think with the right direction she'll do very well," she said.

"So I'm clear what you mean, what do you mean by direction?" Simon asked. "Do you mean I'll need to look over her shoulder and check her work? Because I'm not an expert in marketing by any stretch of the imagination."

"That's not what I meant. Give her a clear brief on what she needs to achieve – results, timings, budget and so on," said Karen

"Okay, I can do that."

About an hour later, Simon asked Angela if she could ask Rebekah to come in and see him. When Rebekah arrived, he could see the worry on her face so set out to reassure her. "Come in and sit down," he motioned for her to sit at the meeting table rather than in front of his desk. She still looked nervous. "Don't worry, you're not in trouble!" She laughed and relaxed. "I know we haven't had much time to sit down and talk about your role."

Her face dropped and he realized his choice of words had been poor, given there was a misconception he was going to make lots of people redundant.

"Over the next few months, the marketing function is going to become more important," he explained. "It means you'll be working more strategically than you have been so far. We'll be launching some new services and we need to get the word out to our target market. I wanted to involve you in the early stages so you can work closely with the departments involved to get the message right. How do you feel about that?"

Rebekah's face lifted. She did her best to hide her sense of relief but it was there for all to see in her expression. "That would be good."

"Now, here's what we're going to do. You might want to write this down." Simon passed her a pen and a sheet of paper and set about explaining what the company had in mind. She looked pensive as she wrote. "What are you initial thoughts?" he asked.

There was a pause.

"You want to know what *I* think?" asked Rebekah, taken aback.

Simon looked puzzled and said, "Yes, that's why I'm asking."

"Okay," she shifted forward on her chair and started to sketch something out on the blank sheet of paper. She turned it round once she was finished. It looked like a process map to Simon. "Before I came here I worked at an events management company for just over a year. This is the process we always used to go through to launch an event. There's a lot to it – it's not just a case of putting on a great training course, there's a lot of planning and work to get delegates there."

Simon smiled to himself as he realized the similarities between this and the dinner party conversation he'd had with Jenny a couple of weeks ago.

"Unless you've got people attending, it doesn't matter how good the content of the course is. What do we know about what people want?" asked Rebekah.

"Andy and I went out to see one of the clients who suggested it yesterday," said Simon.

"Great, what kind of format did they ask for? - you know 'chalk and talk' training versus a hands-on workshop." Simon looked blank. "What about duration? - full day, half day, a couple of hours...?" Simon became uncomfortable. "It's important to know because if people can only get away from their desks for a couple of hours at a time we won't be able to get them to a full day course. What about content?"

This Simon could answer, "They wanted to know more about the functionality of the software so they could use all its features and get their money's worth."

"So which features aren't they using and how would they benefit the client?" Rebekah began to sense that she might have over-stepped the mark and was in danger of annoying Simon with her questions. "How about I think about this and come back to you with a plan?"

Simon nodded, "Sounds like a good idea. Talk to Andy as well; this project is his 'baby'."

If Simon had been watching closely, he would have seen the color drain from Rebekah's cheeks. Unfortunately he didn't notice and was also unaware of the nauseous feeling rising in her stomach.

"I'd go and see him now while it's fresh in your mind," he said.

She kept quiet and clicked the button on the end of her pen repeatedly. Eventually she spoke, "I don't want to bother him with this."

Simon was not impressed, "What do you mean you don't want to bother him? This is an important project and you've got questions which need to be answered. What's the problem?"

She gulped and her eyes started to redden. She was determined not to cry in front of the Managing Director at their first one-to-one meeting. As she started to speak, she was conscious of her voice faltering, "Andy doesn't really listen to me. I've tried to speak to him before about ideas I've had, but he just talks over the top of me. He seems to think I'm just there to write emails for his team to send out, get brochures printed and put adverts in trade magazines. I only ever find out about things at the last minute when there isn't enough time to do a good job or be strategic about what we're doing. I end up fire-fighting all the time and...," her voice started to tail off, "I'm getting really stressed."

Simon had a sense of déjà-vu and realized this conversation reminded him of that evening when Jenny had been upset about her friends not being able to come to her birthday dinner party because she hadn't given them enough time to keep the date free.

If Simon had missed the signs that Rebekah was upset, her raising her hand to her face to brush away a tear woke him up to the situation.

This had gone too far.

He felt like calling Andy into his office and banging their heads together.

He decided to try another angle and truly listen to her. "Okay, let's say hypothetically if Andy wasn't in the office, how else could you find out the information you need to know?"

She sniffed, dried her eyes and started to think. "Well, I suppose I could talk to the salespeople directly."

"Great. What else? Remember this is hypothetical and we're only talking ideas."

"I could speak to some of the clients. Maybe I could put together a survey and send it to clients. I could write down the questions I've got and give them to Andy so he and his team could find out for me!" She smiled.

Which one would you prefer to go with?" asked Simon.

"I think for speed and so I'm not either duplicating work or treading on any toes, it would make sense to write down the questions I've got and give them to Andy, then I can work up a plan and come back to both of you."

"I've got another idea to add in as well: how about you give the questions to me and I'll talk to Andy?"

She let out a sigh and looked relieved, "Would you do that?"

Simon nodded, "Can you get them to me by the end of the day and we'll get this moving?"

Rebekah had a spring in her step when she left his office. "Right," Simon thought to himself, "Now the fun begins. How on earth do I get Andy and Rebekah working together properly?"

Recipe for Market Research

One of the fundamentals of business success is to know and understand your customers so well that you can anticipate what they will want and need to buy. Only by fulfilling their wants and needs can you set up a profitable working relationship.

For decision-makers who are removed from day-to-day interactions with customers, it's important to conduct market research to work out how well your people really know your customers.

Launching a new product without conducting any market research can be like serving up a spicy lamb curry dish for a dinner party when you've never tried cooking it before.

Ingredients:
Cubed lamb, sliced onion, minced onion, yogurt, green chilies, ginger, garlic, ground coriander seeds, ground turmeric, ground cumin seeds, cinnamon, ground mustard seeds and ghee.

Method:
To make the marinade put the chilies, minced onion, spices, ginger and yogurt in a blender or food processor and process until thoroughly mixed – before testing reactions to your product in a focus group or via a questionnaire you need to have the basis of the finished product. People find it difficult to use their imagination so they need help visualizing or imagining using the product. The best spicy dishes use a marinade to tenderize the meat and lock in the flavor. When conducting market research, you may find you need to break down barriers in people's minds about using your product. Although you and your new product development team may believe the product will be the answer your customers' prayers, the customers might not see it. In most markets, the largest proportion of sales are made *after* the early adopters have started using it and it has become mainstream. In this stage of market research, it's all about understanding what customers really want to buy – what do they like / dislike? You may need to test the marinade out on a few friends first before the dinner party. Otherwise, if you're not careful, you could end up with something either too spicy or too bland when serving it up on

the night. Remember that what's right for your taste buds might not suit your guests, so cater for their preferences rather than your own.

Cut the meat into chunks and coat it in the marinade sauce - marinades do not penetrate very deep into the surface of meat, so rather than taking a large piece of meat and expecting it to soak all the way through, cut it into chunks. It's the same with customers. The more you can segment them and treat them as individuals and small groups who think and behave in the same way, the greater the chance of you launching a product which sells well.

Cover and leave overnight in the refrigerator to allow the flavor to soak in – use the 'marinating' process to understand which objections your marketing will need to overcome and how to communicate the benefits of what you're offering. Rather than resisting objections, seek to understand the words and phrases people use when describing what they want. Probe to find out how they use products like yours and how you can make things easier for them.

Add ghee to a pan, lightly fry the onion and do not allow it to brown before adding the lamb and marinade mix – Warm up the market before launching your new product or service. Timing is key so that the market is ready and it not burned out before your product is ready to launch.

Cover and simmer gently for 1½ hours until the meat is tender – While your product is cooking you can build anticipation in the marketplace. Just as the cooking smells will make people feel hungry, you can use marketing, particularly PR messages to make people want what you are about to release to the market.

Serve with rice – By now the customer should be ravenous and ready to eat. Serve up your dish with something bland which doesn't distract them from the main product.

FOOD FOR THOUGHT...

What's it like to work here?

With regard to business strategy, one of the most important things to think about is *Corporate Culture* – even for a one-man band.

We need to think about:
- Our beliefs and ideals
- Our vision and mission
- The sort of leadership do we want
- Is it a business that's built around teamwork
- Do we have a good logo?
- The image of the business
- How flexible and adaptable to be
- The means to handle change management well

Corporate culture is very important because it is around this that you will build your success. Without a good Corporate Culture it's going to be very difficult to grow your business or organization.

Corporate Culture should reach across all the various operational stakeholders:
- Management
- Staff
- Suppliers
- Customers

Corporate Culture also defines:
- How people behave with each other
- How people behave with customers and clients
- How people view their relationships with stakeholders
- How people respond to:
  - Energy use
  - Community involvement
  - Absence from work
  - Work ethic
- How the organization behaves to its employees:
  - Whether to make them more professional
  - Whether to provide training and development

These are all very important aspects of sound management.

Corporate Culture also needs to be driven by the vision and mission of the organization. People who work for the organization need to understand where the organization wants to go in the future and to know how we are going to achieve that and what we are going to do. The people in the organization need to clearly understand the beliefs of the organization.

Corporate culture can be reflected in the attitude and behavior of the leadership. One of the things we have found previously is that people follow the way the leader does things.

The attitude of the people who work in the business is of prime concern, especially what sort of attitude do they have towards the business. One thing we have learnt in business is that you should always hire for attitude – you can teach skills but attitude comes hard wired and you need to make sure that the people's attitude will fit in to the culture of the business you are trying to grow.

You also need to be aware of what image your business is trying to present to the outside world and what people see when they see your business.

Having decided the corporate culture in your business it is important to ensure that the people you engage in your business fit with that culture.

Some examples of different Corporate Cultures

The corporate culture of Virgin, *the Virgin Group*

The sorts of people they hire are often quite young. They are people that are totally committed to the brand. They are people who look up to Sir Richard Branson and see his informal style of doing business. Virgin will hire people to suit that particular culture.

The Body Shop, hire a different type of person:

They are usually people who have attitudes about the environment or about organic products or about the experimentation of cosmetics on animals and so on; they are the sorts of people the Body Shop needs to hire to make that sort of business successful.

McDonald's – yet a different culture:

McDonald's is a totally process driven business. They hire young people mainly in the last three years of their High-Schooling or in their university years. If I am hiring for McDonald's do I want to hire a group of individualists or do I want to hire people that will fit in with the process culture? I will need those people that will fit into the process culture.

Finally, *Nike* - another corporate culture with their label 'Just do it'.

The people that work for Nike are very dedicated to the brand. They would not be seen dead wearing another competitive brand. They are usually young, they are up with the image, they want to wear the clothes and be clearly associated with the brand.

In all four cases we have to have the people with the right attitude for a specific Corporate Culture:

- Virgin with a strong work ethic
- Body Shop with a strong environmental ethic
- McDonalds with a strong process based work ethic
- Nike with a strong brand ethic

The Tale of the Evolution of a Company Culture

Have you ever wondered how a company creates a culture and how it arrives at its current state? Here is a tale that will better assist you to understand the development of a company culture.

Start with a cage containing five apes. In the cage, hang a banana on a string and put stairs under it. Before long, an ape will go up the stairs and start to climb towards the banana. As soon as he touches the stairs, spray all of the apes with cold water. After a while, another ape will make an attempt with the same result, that all the apes will be sprayed with cold water. This continues through several attempts. Pretty soon, when another ape tries to climb the stairs, the other apes will try to prevent it.

Now, turn off the cold water. Remove one ape from the cage and replace it with a new one.

The new ape sees the banana and wants to climb the stairs. To his horror, all the other apes attack him. After another attempt and attack he knows that if he tries to climb the stairs he will be assaulted.

Next, remove another of the original five apes and replace it with a new one. The newcomer goes to the stairs and is attacked. The previous newcomer takes part in the punishment with enthusiasm.

Again replace a third original ape with a new one. The new one makes it to the stairs and is attacked as well. Two of the four apes that beat him have no idea why they are not permitted to climb the stairs, or why they are participating in beating the newest ape.

After replacing the fourth and fifth original apes, all the apes that have been sprayed with cold water have been replaced.

Nevertheless, no ape ever again approaches the stairs.

FIND OUT MORE...

For more tips, tools and resources go to:
www.businesscookerybook.com/resources

Chapter 6

The day after the exhibition, Jenny started going through the multitude of brochures she had collected in her bag. She realized that if she was going to target this section of the market, she would need to review her suppliers. The companies and contractors she was currently using were great and good to work with, however she wasn't sure that they would be suitable if she landed a large hotel contract. It would be best if she began to develop links with other suppliers so that she could hit the ground running when the right kind of work did come in.

She started to go through the exhibition brochure page by page visiting websites to see the full range of products and services available. She had her own particular flavor of design – modern yet quirky, so focused on the companies who had those kinds of design elements in their products or could show that kind of work in their portfolio.

Finding suppliers was easier than finding contractors. With a product you know what you're getting. You can see it, touch it get a sense of how it will fit into your design. Choosing contractors concerned her more. Whenever you're buying services they represent your company and your personal reputation when they're doing work on your behalf. There's a high level of trust involved.

She'd had her fingers burned in the past when she'd taken new contractors at their word, particularly on residential work, and they had over-run, grossly underestimated the labor charges or left the site in a mess at the end of the day. Now being older and wiser, she would take much greater care. She would work with contractors based on recommendations rather than slick advertisements. Jenny decided that one way of doing this would be to visit some of the suppliers and ask who they used or had heard were reliable.

Talking to her mum the other day had served to remind her how important it was to ask for advice from the right people. As her mum put it, "You wouldn't ask a life-long vegetarian for tips on cooking roast beef – it'd be based purely on speculation or guesswork".

Jenny's mind was made up; she'd talk to the suppliers who sold the kinds of products she would be using in her designs and ask their advice. Some of the products she wanted to use were quite specialized. Jenny smiled as she took the food theme further, "I suppose it's like when you buy a new ingredient for a dish in a market, you'd ask the person you buy it from how you cook it, if you need any special equipment and how you prepare it," her train of thought continued. "And in an expensive restaurant, there are specialists cooking different dishes - like the pastry chef. You have to find the people who are experts at what they do."

In the afternoon she took the car and visited two local suppliers and got names and numbers from them, as well as samples and brochures for her files.

While she was driving and negotiating a tricky junction, her mobile phone rang. She resisted the temptation to answer it. Her children often told her off for talking on the phone while driving and she knew she shouldn't do it. At school they had been told it was wrong and they'd seen it on TV, so it frightened them when they saw her doing it but all they ever heard in response was, "Shh...Mummy needs to talk to someone about work" as she pressed the button on her hands-free kit.

This time it was impossible to answer it. She let it go to voicemail. A few minutes later the phone rang again with the message.

She huffed and pulled off the main road into a side-street and parked, concerned it might be the school calling her. Instead she heard a new voice, "Hi this is a message for Jenny Richardson," she remembered she really needed to set up a proper greeting on her phone – the robotic voice giving her number but not her name or business simply wouldn't do – one of the challenges of using the same phone for work and personal use. "This is Tony Rossi; we met yesterday at the exhibition. Could you call me back please on..." She fumbled in her handbag for a pen and missed the number. Fortunately her voicemail allowed her to press a button to return the call, which she did.

The conversation with Tony was brief. Could she come into their office in the next few days for a chat? Yes, of course she could. As she continued her car journey she wondered what Tony wanted to talk to her about and even allowed herself to get a little excited and hopeful.

When she got home she set about gathering together the photos from the hotel and the other projects she had worked on recently. She mounted them into a small portfolio which would fit into her bag. She wanted to be able to tuck it away, just in case he hadn't expected to look at her work. She still wasn't exactly sure what the purpose of the meeting was.

Later that week, Jenny arrived at Tony's office. As she walked in through the door, she could see it was a spacious studio so wasn't surprised when he grabbed his coat and suggested going to the coffee shop over the road rather than have their meeting in the office.

Once settled with their drinks, Tony thanked her for coming along at such short notice. He gave her a brief history of the firm, which he had founded nine years ago, and explained the kind of work they did. Then he asked her about her career history and the type of projects she had been involved in. It seemed an appropriate time to bring out her portfolio. They shuffled their chairs so they were both side by side to go through the pages together as she explained each in turn. Tony remained quiet and nodded his head as she talked while he held his chin thoughtfully.

When she had reached the end, he said, "I'm really glad you brought this along. It helps me get a sense of what you can do. Shall we get to the point?"

"Sure," said Jenny.

"One of my team is going on maternity leave in a couple of months, so we'll be looking for someone to cover her. She handles the interior design element of what we do. We specialize in bars, restaurants and some hotels, so when you told me you had an interest in hotels and had some experience that got my attention. Because we're a small team, it's important we find someone who's going to fit in. It's not the place for *prima donnas*, so I like that you're down to earth and seem to have a good personality. I also like the design work you've done. Most of our clients are after a modern and unique look – something that will help them stand out and get people talking. I realize you've got your own business and you're probably busy already, but how would you feel about maybe helping us with one or two projects over the next six to twelve months?"

She did her best not to jump for joy and tried to appear professional, "I'm sure I could accommodate that."

Tony looked slightly disappointed so she continued, "Only kidding, I'd LOVE to!" and beamed. Tony was relieved and Jenny realized she could actually be herself around him and it was okay. She was going to enjoy working with his company.

"Great." He reached into his inside jacket pocket, pulled out his mobile phone and dialed. She could faintly hear a woman's voice answer. "Nicole, could you join us over at the coffee shop please? Thanks. See you in a minute." He put the phone away, "Nicole's our designer. I'd like you meet her."

A few minutes later a woman entered the coffee shop and Jenny rose to greet her, "You must be Nicole," she glanced down, "the bump gave it away!" Nicole smiled.

"Thanks for coming over Nicole," said Simon. "This is Jenny. I've just been talking to Jenny about helping out with some of the projects you're working on in the run-up to your maternity leave and covering for you while you're away. Jenny's been freelancing for about a year, but she was a designer for a number of years before taking time out for her kids."

They continued to talk for another twenty minutes before arranging a time for Jenny to come back and spend the day with Nicole so she could be brought up to speed on the projects.

Jenny couldn't believe her luck! She didn't normally call Simon in the office, but she couldn't help herself, "Darling, you're not going to believe what just happened..."

Giving Rebekah's questions to Andy turned out to be easier than Simon had expected. Andy looked at the list and while he was still reading muttered, "Good questions." Simon left him to mull them over.

Andy put the list down, sat back in his office chair, put his hands behind his head and stared at the ceiling. He took a few deep breaths. His mind was racing as he considered what Rebekah had asked. He realized there was more to this than he had initially thought. He also quietly realized that because Rebekah was asking questions he thought were obvious, maybe expecting her to pick up information by osmosis wasn't going to be the best approach going forward.

He filled his lungs, rocked forward, grabbed the list, jumped up from his chair and gathered his team around him. He asked his assistant Grace to call Rebekah and get her to join him and his team for an impromptu meeting.

Grace wondered what was going on and while she was on the phone, listened to the chatter in the office. Was there going to be some sort of announcement? She grabbed her phone from her bag and under the desk rapidly typed out a message to Angela, Simon's PA: *A just asked me 2 get R! Thought they werent talking. Wots going on? Keep you posted G x*

Rebekah did her best to hide her concern as she walked into the sales area and saw all the team sat staring at her. Andy smiled and asked her to sit down in the empty seat.

"Thanks everyone, I know you're busy today. As some of you know, we're going to start running open training courses for our clients. It's a great opportunity to get to know them better and it gives you something you can add on to the sale for new clients and existing clients. Rebekah's going to be looking after the marketing and so she needs to get the answers to some questions. I want all of you to work with Rebekah and help her to understand our key clients as well as you do. The better the information you give her, the better the marketing she can do for you and the easier it's going to be for you to sell the courses. Okay everyone?"

The team looked at each other; a few shrugged their shoulders while others nodded. No one volunteered any objections or questions, so Andy continued, "Fantastic. Okay you can get back to work now."

Some swiveled around on their chairs to face their desks again.

Some jumped up and walked back to their desks.

Some took the opportunity to take a cigarette break – Grace was one of the first to grab her bag and head for the door. Andy knew that as soon as they were outside, the speculation would begin. He couldn't stop people talking and communication was healthy for a team - wasn't it?

"Rebekah," he leaned his head towards his office door and she followed him in. "Sit down," he pointed his hand towards the chair in front of his desk. "Some really good questions here; you've really thought about this, haven't you?" She nodded. "Okay, so the team is on board with helping you. What's the best way of going about this?"

Rebekah gulped and dropped her eyes into her lap where she held her notes. "Um...there are some uh questions that are just facts that I need, so could we err go through the ones you can answer right now?" Andy leaned forward and nodded quickly three times. He held the list of questions in front of him. "To answer some of these questions we'll need to ask a few of the clients, you know, to see which answers are most popular - like how long the course should be and which day of the week is easiest for them to do."

Over a period of half an hour Andy and Rebekah worked through the questions, answering those that they could and formulating a questionnaire to give to the team. They agreed on when the information needed to be collected by and when Rebekah would come back with a plan. They also agreed that they would give it a week to get the important questions answered and make decisions based on what they found.

Andy had a feeling the research would simply confirm what he already thought about the courses, but he decided to humor Rebekah by biting his tongue and not saying so. He figured letting Rebekah have her say would help his relationship and increase his influence with Simon.

In the week between their meeting and Rebekah reporting back to Andy with her plan she, Karen, Andy and Simon met to organize the logistics of putting on an event. Karen had organized training courses in the past and continued to do so and Rebekah's background in event marketing stood her in good stead. Andy and Simon were the 'newbies' so Rebekah and Karen were at the same time educating them about what was possible, what wasn't and why some things had to be done a certain way. In the absence of information from the clients about duration of courses and what they wanted to learn, there was still a lot that could be organized.

Karen made recommendations on suitable trainers. The people in their technical support team were fantastic while in their comfort zone and yet she wasn't sure how they would respond to a request to run group training courses. Apparently they were operating at capacity anyway so probably couldn't take the time out. She suggested in the meantime that a professional trainer could be taught the software so they could run the course.

There would probably be no need to find a training venue because the office had access to a large meeting room which was fully-equipped with all the facilities that would be needed. It would depend on how many people booked. They made initial enquiries into catering companies, but until they knew how long the course would be, it was impossible to make a final decision.

The big question was around content for the course. The possibilities were endless because the software could be used in so many different ways. Until a decision was made on what the course was about, Rebekah would have to hold back on creating marketing materials – something she took care to remind everyone whenever she was given the chance. She didn't want to risk being accused of delivering late if she hadn't been able to brief the design agency in good time. However, she often felt what she was saying went in one ear and out of the other when she heard comments like, "We can finalize the content a few days in advance" or "We'll see who books places and then write the content around them". Couldn't they see that without knowing what the course was about, no one would book a place?

Rebekah did her best to hold in her frustration when she was in meetings, but when she got home at night her boyfriend Sam knew something was bothering her. She'd offered to cook dinner. She was tired, so opened the freezer, took out frozen pies and slid them into the oven.

Rebekah set the timer for twenty minutes and went to get changed out of her work clothes into her comfy clothes. She felt fresher when she heard the beep sounding in the kitchen. She started cooking the vegetables and re-set the timer to go off after a further ten minutes. She turned on the TV in the kitchen and she stayed with the boiling pans as she caught up with the day's events on the news. When the timer had a few minutes to go she turned on the kettle to make gravy. As the water boiled, the beeper went off again. She grabbed the oven glove, opened the oven, picked up the tray and saw frozen pies. "Huh?"

Sam came into the kitchen to help serve up and looked puzzled, "Isn't the cooker working?" She checked the settings and realized she'd turned the internal light and fan on but not the temperature dial on the electric oven. He knew he shouldn't laugh, but he did. Rebekah threw down the oven gloves and stormed out, "Well if you think it's so funny, YOU can cook dinner!"

Sam heard the pounding of her steps as she headed for the bedroom. He could picture her now throwing herself dramatically on the bed and half-heartedly he decided to follow her.

"Lighten up Bek," he said. "Everyone makes mistakes." She huffed and buried her head in the pillow. "You don't seem yourself tonight. You're usually so organized. What's wrong?" He stroked her arm to coax her from her hiding place beneath the pillow and eventually her face peeped out.

"It's not the dinner," she sat up and folded her arms. "I'm stressed out at work. They've finally given me a decent project to work on but they don't seem to realize that if you don't start planning the marketing early enough it won't be ready to go when everything else is."

"Like the pies!" he joked.

She stopped, stared into space and said, "Yes. Exactly like the pies." In an almost trance-like state she got up and walked past him. He followed her to the living room where she pulled her notepad from her bag and started making notes. "Thank you," she said. "I know what I need to do about work now."

He reached into his pocket and checked the contents of his wallet, "Forget the pies, shall we get pizza?" "Deal."

Recipe for Sourcing Suppliers

Whatever product or service we are providing there are going to be many things that make it up. There may be physical or intellectual input from you combined with physical and intellectual input from others. A good example here is a car. It is put together by the manufacturer using a wide range of component parts provided by others.

What is firstly important here is the input from the manufacturer creating the design of the car and the various attributes it has. Different models will be produced to suit different tastes, needs and price points. Next the manufacturer must consider which component suppliers will provide parts that meet our quality standards in the timeframes they require. Another example here is computer manufacturers who use a range of OEM (Original Equipment Manufacturer) parts put together in a certain way within a shell designed by them.

In business we need to concentrate on what we do well and leave others to do what they do best. Often training suppliers work out course profiles, sell them to customers but sub-contact the work to training associates who deliver the courses - somewhat like getting caterers in or buying pre-prepared food which you then present as your own creation!

Ingredients:
Pre-prepared food from deli or food store. Additional ingredients to make dish we wish to present.

Method:
Based on guests to be fed chose pre-prepared food that will meet their taste requirements – pick something that is going to suit all tastes and the theme of the meal desired. Remember to be mindful of special requirements.

Work out what other ingredients you require to help make the meal special and with your particular stamp on it – it may be the way you are going to cook the rice that is going to make the meal special.

Think about the presentation of the meal – what plates and bowls we use can impact on how the guest experiences the meal. This also applies to our business customers. For example, look at how perfume is marketed – which is more important the packaging or the scent?

Work out which aspects of the food experience you want to emphasize – Nearly all top class restaurants put their food on plain white crockery so as to emphasize the presentation of the actual meal itself. Obviously the crockery used is often from a well known supplier. We need to make sure we know what we want to emphasize to our customers. and that the suppliers we use enhance the delivery of that message.

FOOD FOR THOUGHT...

Have a "Kaizen" philosophy throughout your business

Some people say that if you're not failing at something then you're not learning or moving forward. There is some truth to this, but we are certainly not suggesting that you deliberately set out to fail just to learn important things.

Everyone makes mistakes along the way, and sometimes this will go wrong no matter how hard you try to make them go right. When this happens, you have two choices: shrug your shoulders and move on without caring, or learn from the experience so you can improve your processes and systems.

That's what "Kaizen" is all about.

It is a philosophy of business that emphasizes constant improvement; in fact, it truly requires constant improvement as the foundation of the entire business model. This approach is prevalent in most Japanese companies, and is a big part of why they have been so successful over the last few decades both in terms of product sales and product reliability.

Many people think Kaizen is about focused on fixing problems so they don't happen again. While this is of course part of the process, it is not the central or primary focus of Kaizen. Instead, the Kaizen philosophy emphasizes that even when things are going well and proceeding smoothly, there are still lessons to be earned and improvements to be made.

When your business has a Kaizen approach, you and your team pay a great deal of attention to fixing problems and learning from them when things go wrong.

With Kaizen, you and your team will be paying even more attention to looking at things that are going very well and asking yourselves "How can we do this even better?"

We need to make sure that our employees and everybody involved in the business has this Kaizen type perspective. If we make a big sale is not a matter of looking in the mirror and saying what a good job we did, what we need to do is look in the mirror and say:

"How can we do this good job even better?"

The key question to ask yourself every day is: "What can we do better today than we did yesterday?" In this way you will be building innovation and continuous learning into your business and if there is an obligation on all staff to think in this way it can have an almost exponential impact on your business.

FIND OUT MORE...

For more tips, tools and resources go to:
www.businesscookerybook.com/resources

Chapter 7

It was an overcast, miserable morning. One of those days when you long for the sun to peep out from behind the clouds to lift your mood. Today Jenny didn't need to rely on sunshine to feel excited because she was on her way to meet with Nicole and learn about the projects she was working on. She turned the radio up loud in the car and each time she stopped at traffic lights, she danced in her seat. Well, that's if you can really call it dancing because she kept her hands and arms low so she wouldn't be spotted by anyone!

She arrived at her destination and parked the car. Jenny was welcomed into the office and sat down at Nicole's table, ready to start. She could hear music playing in the background and as she looked around the walls she saw framed photos of buildings and interiors. "Are these all projects you've worked on?" Jenny asked Nicole, who replied that they were. Nicole took the opportunity to explain more about each photograph and how they had worked on the buildings featured in them.

For the rest of the day Nicole took Jenny through all of the internal processes at TVR Associates and how they usually managed projects. Over the coming months, Jenny would be shadowing Nicole once a week so she would be able to take over from her when Nicole's maternity leave started. Until then, Jenny would still need to have projects of her own. Jenny got the impression that Nicole still intended to do some work from home while on maternity leave and see certain projects through to completion. This was Nicole's first child and Jenny wondered how much things would change when the baby arrived. Noah had been a difficult baby and there would have been no way for her to work as well as look after him. Nicole's baby might be different.

Jenny resolved to continue to develop her own business and have her own suppliers and contractors in place.

During the drive back after her day with Nicole, Jenny's mood had changed from eager optimism to grounded realism and she knew she would need to improve her all-round business skills in order to get clients of her own.

The idea of going back through all the emails Debbie had sent her about marketing her business filled her with dread. She just didn't know where to start. She felt a knot in her stomach when she thought about her commitment to getting PR for the hotel she had refurbished. Time was ticking along and if they wanted to be featured in any magazines, they really needed to be working on it now. She assumed, correctly, that monthly magazines plan out their main articles four to six month in advance and in some case even up to a year in advance.

Jenny didn't want to keep running back to her mum each time she needed business advice and she remembered that in the days when she tried to get to every small business networking event going, there were a number of organizations who arranged workshops and training courses on marketing and PR.

She pulled up outside her friend's house a few streets away from hers. She had met Clare at the school gate three years ago when dropping Noah off in the mornings. Clare had once helped her stop Rosie running into the road after breaking free from Jenny's grasp and they had remained friends ever since.

She rang the doorbell. In the background she could hear the sound of children's voices. Clare answered and had to put her leg in front of her dog Pixie to stop her getting out of the house. "Hi Jenny," Clare said, "come in." She grabbed Pixie's collar and pulled her back inside to let Jenny enter.

"Noah! Rosie! Your mum's here!" Clare called out.

"Thank you so much for looking after them for me," said Jenny. "I'm sorry I'm a bit later than I said I would be."

"Don't worry about it," said Clare. "They've been busy playing with Jake and Mikey." Jake and Mikey were Clare's two sons. Jake, the elder boy, was very boisterous and quite a handful and if Jenny was honest, she thought Mikey was a bit of an attention-seeking cry-baby, but she'd never have said either of those things to her friend's face. She was grateful Clare had offered to look after Noah and Rosie while she had her meeting with Nicole and felt a bit guilty for judging her children.

Later that evening, after Jenny had made dinner, bathed the children and put them to bed before Simon came home, she had some time to think more about the issue of publicity for her business and the hotel. She checked her email for old messages from the people who organized the networking events. They were out of date now so she clicked through to their websites to see whether there were any suitable events coming up. She spotted one which caught her eye. It was a 'women in business' conference and it looked like they had an interesting line-up of speakers talking about growing your business. The ticket was affordable and the event was happening in a few weeks time, so she reserved her place.

She turned her attention to the processes she would need to have in place to manage the projects for Nicole and also her own projects, assuming she was able to secure some.

She heard the front door open and close. Simon was home. She called to him from her study, "I'm in here darling."

He walked through, took off his coat and kissed her. "It's rotten weather out there. The rain's really coming down."

"Good day?" Jenny asked.

"Not bad," he replied. "Things seem to be moving along nicely with the course. Andy and Rebekah are even working together on the marketing!"

"That's good. I know they'd been stressing you out. Actually, I've just booked myself on a conference to learn more about marketing," Jenny said.

"Hmm... sounds like a good idea. How did your day with the architects go?" he asked. Jenny explained and told him how she'd still need to get her own clients. She added that she'd have a lot of work on her hands if she did land her own project and had to work on some of Nicole's at the same time.

"Can't Debbie help you?" he asked. "That's what you pay her for, isn't it?"

Jenny was thoughtful. Usually she just used Debbie for administrative work as needed, but more recently Debbie had come up with some good ideas for the business, so maybe she could help with project management too. "I hadn't thought of that," said Jenny. "I'll see if she's able to come over and see me soon. I'll ask her what she thinks and if she agrees, I'll train her up. Dinner's in the kitchen, by the way."

Simon nodded and headed for the kitchen. He'd been working late again and was starving hungry.

The following morning Rebekah was the one to call the update meeting on the courses. She had spent three hours the night before preparing Gantt charts and flow charts to show all of the various elements of the campaign for the training courses. She couldn't understand why she hadn't thought of it before, so perhaps the pie incident had been a blessing in disguise.

Simon and Andy looked on with interest and Karen could only listen through the speaker phone because today was officially one of her days off. Rebekah did her best to describe to Karen what she was showing to the others, "It's a bit like cooking a meal. There are some things that take longer than others or you need to get someone else to prepare them separately. If you don't get them started and into the oven, they won't be ready when you're ready to serve up the other parts of the meal. Think of it like cooking a roast dinner, you can't put the meat into the oven at the same time as you boil the vegetables and expect it all to be done in five minutes. Even if you put it in the oven at the highest heat, it'd be cooked on the outside but as soon as you carved it you'd see it was raw, bloody and inedible. You'd end up throwing it away. If we don't make a decision soon, the marketing for the course will turn out that way - overdone because we're having to hard-sell to get people to book and leaving a bad taste in our clients' mouths. You wouldn't eat again at a restaurant that gave you food poisoning and you'd feel sick whenever you thought about going there. We don't want our clients to think of us like that."

Simon was stunned that the cooking analogy was coming up again! "This is spooky," he thought to himself.

Rebekah's point was well-made and everyone 'got' what she was trying to communicate. The marketing needed to be kept on a low heat to avoid alienating their clients and given more time to cook so it left people curious about the courses rather than pressured into booking. It made sense.

"I hear what you're saying Rebekah," Simon said. "Right, let's make some decisions so she can get on and get the marketing briefed to the agency. Rebekah, Andy how is the customer research coming along?"

"Thanks Simon and thanks Andy for all your help and your team's help in getting this together so quickly," Rebekah continued to explain the findings and made recommendations on the topic and the duration that most people were interested in.

She was pleasantly surprised when Andy added in his comments, "I'm really glad we did this research because we did get some unexpected results. If we'd have gone with what we thought people wanted we'd have had a tough time selling it. My team has already told me their clients enjoyed being asked and feeling they were a part of shaping the courses. Sanjay, who looks after one of the bigger accounts, said that he was going to work with his contact to put together a business case for them investing in the course. If we can get all our people working as the users' allies, it's going to make this a doddle to sell!"

"Andy," Rebekah said, "what kinds of resources does Sanjay need for the business case? Maybe we can get some special reports and white papers written for all the team to use."

"That'd be good," said Andy. "Shall we talk offline?"

Simon was impressed. Within a short space of time, Andy's attitude had really changed. He and Rebekah were working much better together. Karen was being included in meetings. He would have a lot to talk to his coach about when he met with Sasha for his next session. Maybe she'd been right when she said told him he had a resourceful team around him and to empower them to make their own decisions. Over the past few weeks he had been working hard on his active listening skills. Until recently he had prided himself on being a good listener; after all, he could retain a great deal of information and repeat back to people what they had said (a skill he relied heavily on when Jenny accused him of not listening to her while he was watching sport on TV at home). Yet he now realized hearing and repeating wasn't necessarily the same as listening and understanding.

Over the course of the following two weeks, Rebekah worked hard with the design and marketing agency to get a good plan together. She felt much more at ease approaching both Simon and Andy when she needed more information and found the more she shared with them about how she was getting on and the ideas the agency came up with, the more involved they wanted to be. On the one hand this was a good thing because they were taking more personal ownership of the project, on the other she realized she would need to take care they didn't try to take over or meddle in areas they knew nothing about.

As the thought crossed her mind, she checked herself. Was she being arrogant? She hadn't been there long and maybe they did know more about the company, the customers and what got a response from them. Yes, she knew about event marketing, had a keen interest in social media and had a marketing diploma, but did this mean she couldn't learn anything from them?

She felt embarrassed when she thought about how people might have seen her when she joined. She started to cringe when she remembered that big stand-off with Andy only 10 days into her new job. Things had blown up in her face when she committed to advertising in a particular trade magazine when according to Andy, "None of our customers read that rag. It's rubbish". She'd felt compelled to hold her ground and argue the point when maybe she should have listened more or sought his involvement sooner. She let out a long sigh and felt her body relax. Was her boyfriend Sam right when he'd told her to 'lighten up'? Maybe she should.

Her train of thought was interrupted when the phone rang beside her. She recognized the number as belonging to Melanie, their Account Manager at the agency. "Hi Mel," she said.

"Hi Bek. I've just emailed the document over to you. I think we're there, so can you have a quick look while we're on the phone?" Rebekah opened the email and they went through it with a fine-toothed comb. The presentation to the directors was scheduled for 8.30am the next morning, so it needed to be right. Rebekah was excited and nervous at the same time. She hoped and prayed the plan would be approved without a hitch. Realistically, the key people had been involved all the way along, so it should just be a case of giving it the final sign-off. Nonetheless, she transferred the file to a USB stick and went to Simon's office.

"Hi Simon, got a minute?" She could see he was gathering papers together into his case and looked as though he was preparing to leave the office.

He nodded and continued to pack, "I've got about five minutes. Shoot." As he did the gun gesture he felt like an idiot and immediately regretted it. Rebekah was bemused. "As you know we've got the agency coming in tomorrow morning to present the plan," stated Rebekah. "I wanted to give you the chance to look at it overnight in case you've got any questions in the morning."

Simon was pleasantly surprised. "Maybe people are starting to understand how I like to work," he thought as she handed him the USB stick and left. In their last coaching session, Sasha had explained to him how everyone learns and processes information differently. They had established that he liked to read, mull things over and then talk it through, rather than be asked to comment on something he'd only just seen and hadn't had a chance to think about.

At home that evening, Simon reviewed the document he had been given. While he did have some questions, he was pleased with what was being presented. Rebekah had done a good job at consolidating the salient points and briefing the agency to come up with a plan which was a very good fit for what they were trying to achieve. There were some ideas in there that he was seeing for the first time, particularly around using social media to spread the word and using existing technologies to handle ticket bookings and payments. For a software company he reflected that they didn't make the best use of software themselves. They were still reliant on headcount and it hadn't occurred to him that so much of the e-mail campaign, online marketing, booking and payment processes could be automated. He was intrigued and instead of dreading sitting through an agency presentation, he was quite looking forward to it.

At 8.15a.m. Simon half-expected to be the first one in the office and it seemed that way as he walked through. When he reached the meeting room it was a different story. All the directors were assembled and tucking into Danish pastries while the Account Manager and Account Director from the agency made small talk. He could see that their presentation was already loaded with the first slide ready to go.

Rebekah rose from her chair and made the appropriate introductions. "Hmm...good firm handshake," Simon thought as he shook the Account Director's hand. He was never sure how tightly to grip a woman's hand when he shook it. Should he shake it the same as a man - where if he was honest with himself, it was sometimes a test of strength and dominance - or be gentler? He'd been guilty of nearly crushing the tiny hand of one of his female suppliers in the past. It was a potential minefield - or was he being over-the-top? He heard his name being called and it jolted him back to where he was.

Karen was offering him a pecan pastry. If only he'd known about the treats before he had his breakfast. He patted his tummy and shook his head. She smiled and shrugged, "More for us then."

He glanced up at the wall clock: 8.27am. He looked around and did a name-check in his head. Yes, everyone was here. "Thanks for joining us today. Shall we get started?" He looked in Rebekah's direction.

She took the signal and started the meeting by giving a short background, explained who the visitors were, how long they'd be presenting for and the objectives of the meeting. Everyone agreed on the objectives and added one or two of their own, but in a nutshell it was to sign off on the marketing plan and decide on the logistics of promoting the event and taking bookings.

The meeting went very well. The agency kept to the time they'd been allocated and allowed plenty of opportunities to answer queries as they came up. Because he'd had time to prepare questions, Simon felt he was able to make a real contribution to the meeting and clarify his understanding of how everything would work. Both Andy and Karen seemed to have well-thought-out questions and constructive comments to make. Even Diane the Finance Director had good questions about the amount they'd budgeted for and how that would translate into sales, and then profit. He wondered if Rebekah had also given them the presentation to look at the previous evening. If she had, it wasn't a bad strategy. Perhaps she was a bit of dark horse. Rebekah had involved everyone from the start, shown she'd listened to them, made them feel important by giving them the chance to review the presentation and also given them time to consider their thoughts on it. Nice one Rebekah!

The agency circulated timing plans which fitted in perfectly with the Gantt charts Rebekah had presented a few days earlier. This was a different experience of working with an agency. In his previous role, the relationship with consultants had been strained at best, with them forever trying to get the company to adapt to their processes rather than the other way around. These people seemed to have listened and were seeing it as more like a partnership than a client/agency relationship. A bit like having an external marketing department.

As they finished their presentation, Melanie the Account Manager said, "I think we've got all the ingredients we need to make this an amazing lunch," she corrected herself, "I mean launch!" and everyone smiled. Rebekah must have told her about the analogy she'd used to get everyone to see how important it was to get the marketing into the oven and start cooking. Simon wondered if he could take the cooking theme further and use it to help all the staff get on board with where the company was going. He made a note of it. His coaching session with Sasha was that afternoon and he wanted to discuss the internal communications with her.

Recipe for Systems and Processes

Many things in business require forward planning and marshalling of a range of resources. It is important that we give ourselves enough time to make good strategic decisions. We therefore need to ensure that we are concentrating on those areas that require our particular attention and letting others do the rest. The questions arise "what should I be doing?" and "what can I delegate?"

The timing of making decisions is also of great importance. In the following recipe it is best that we do some of the cooking in advance and part of the cooking at the time of serving. The lamb shanks are better cooked the night before so that it can be reheated and the fat removed. The flavor will also be enhanced.

Ingredients:
Lamb shanks, plain flour for dusting, sea salt, freshly ground black pepper, olive oil, red onions, chopped rosemary, cloves of garlic, balsamic vinegar, red wine.

Method:
Preheat oven to 150C/300F/gas mark 2 – You need to create an environment where the likelihood of success is high. Selecting the right heat is important to the outcome of the recipe as is logistics, delegation and automation in a business.

Dust the shanks in the flour seasoned with salt and pepper – In many cases we need to ensure that we are in the right state before we start allocating tasks to various team members.

In a heavy casserole dish heat the oil, brown shanks on all sides then remove – it is important to see that we have a well rounded team that is properly equipped to be used for the task.

Lower the heat, add the onions and cook for another couple of minutes – There may be people who are vital to the project (like onions are to the taste of a casserole).

Raise the heat, add the balsamic vinegar and red wine and reduce for a couple of minutes – these particular ingredients will make the dish have its own special taste and this will depend on the quantities used. Delegating tasks to the right people who have the special qualities needed or the right personalities will have a significant impact on the results achieved.

Return the shanks to the pan, reduce the heat and cover with a piece of moistened greaseproof paper and the lid. Cook in oven for about 2 ½ hours or alternatively on a low heat on the hob – Some things just take time and cannot be rushed. In other situations you need to take the heat out of the situation before proceeding.

Check shanks from time to time, basting with the juices. Serve whole with oniony juices. Add vegetables to suit but great with mashed potatoes – When you delegate tasks it is important to occasionally check that what you think is happening is actually happening. It has been said that you need to *inspect* as well as *expect*.

FOOD FOR THOUGHT...

Do you need a shark in your tank?

The Japanese have always liked fresh fish. But the waters near Japan have not held may fish for decades. So to feed the Japanese population, fishing boats got bigger and went farther than ever.

The farther the fishermen went, the longer it took to bring in the fish. If the return trip took more than a few days, the fish were not fresh. The Japanese did not like the taste.

To solve this problem, fishing companies installed freezers on their boats. They would catch the fish and freeze them at sea. Freezers allowed the boats to go farther and stay longer.

However, the Japanese could taste the difference between fresh and frozen and they did not like frozen fish. The frozen fish brought a lower price. So fishing companies installed fish tanks.

They would catch the fish and stuff them in the tanks fin to fin. After a little thrashing around, the fish stopped moving. They were tired and dull, but alive.

Unfortunately, the Japanese could still taste the difference. Because the fish did not move for days, they lost their fresh fish taste. The Japanese preferred the lively taste of fresh fish, not sluggish fish. So how did the Japanese fishing companies solve this problem? How do they get fresh fish to Japan? If you were consulting the fish industry, what would you recommend?

How Japanese Fish Stay Fresh: To keep the fish tasting fresh, the Japanese fishing companies still put fish in the tanks. But now they add a small shark to each tank.

The shark eats a few fish, but most fish arrive in a very lively state. The fish are challenged.

Both we and our businesses become tired and dull at times, so we need a shark in our lives to keep us awake and moving?

Often a recession will provide such a shark and if we are intelligent, persistent and competent we should come out of it with stronger businesses. Maybe every so often we should set greater challenges for ourselves to conquer and look at ways in which we will be able to meet those new challenges. Maybe we need a coach or consultant to help see things in new ways?

FIND OUT MORE...

For more tips, tools and resources go to:
www.businesscookerybook.com/resources

Chapter 8

Jenny heard a knock on the front door and glanced at her watch. Was it that time already? She opened the door to Debbie and invited her in.

She'd talked to Debbie on the phone about taking on more responsibility in the business and she had agreed, so the meeting today was to train Debbie to help with project management.

Simon had talked to Jenny about some of the cooking analogies people in his office had been using. He said they'd made things much easier to digest and laughed when he realized the pun. "Well," she'd thought to herself, "if something like that can work in a big business, maybe it can work in a small business too." She decided to give it a try with Debbie.

"Thanks for coming over Debbie. It's going to be much easier to train you on this if I can show it to you, rather than talking about it over the phone." Jenny paused before continuing. "I suppose it's like the difference between someone giving you instructions on how to cook a meal over the phone compared to helping you in the kitchen and showing you how."

"I know what you mean," said Debbie and she smiled. "Actually I called my mum last week for the recipe for a birthday cake for my son. She always used to make the most fantastic cakes when I was a kid. I wrote everything down while we were on the phone - I got the ingredients, the order to mix it in and how long to cook it for. I honestly thought I'd got it. A few days later I followed the recipe and made the cake - so I thought! I put it in at the right temperature and for the right time and left it. I came back and it was burned to a crisp! It took a while to figure out what went wrong." Jenny looked curious, so Debbie explained, "I've got a fan assisted electric oven and Mum always made the cake in a gas oven. She didn't know and I forgot to mention it. I just looked up gas mark 4 on a conversion table to see what it would be for my oven. If she'd been in the kitchen and seen it, she'd have told me to turn the heat down, but over the phone she just didn't know."

Jenny could see how drawing analogies with cooking really did work – Debbie 'got' what she was talking about straight away!

Jenny went on to explain that with project management it was like running a restaurant. There had to be a process in place for seating the diners, taking their order and then making sure everyone's food came out at the same time. The kinds of projects she would be working on would be like catering for a party of twelve who all ordered different main courses. No matter whether they had ordered something quick and easy like a salad or something which had to be marinated overnight, it still needed to be served together. The diner only tended to see what happened in the restaurant, yet all the staff knew there was so much more to it going on behind the scenes in the kitchen. The trick with project managing interior design was to co-ordinate a multitude of resources while making everything as painless as possible for the client.

Straight away Debbie started using the analogy herself asking whether she would be taking on the role of Maître D' (mainly client-facing and dealing with customer service), Head Chef (working behind the scenes and managing the contractors) or a combination of both.

Good question, Jenny thought. After consideration, she decided Debbie's role would be Head Chef while Jenny took charge of the Maître D's role as well as that of waiting staff - Jenny would welcome new clients, take the orders, i.e. take a brief from them and make recommendations, take the order to the kitchen and then bring it to the client when ready to serve.

Jenny took time to show Debbie how to use the project management software she used and gave her details of all the contractors and suppliers she was thinking of using.

The whole process took about four hours and they were both getting to the point where they were becoming tired. Although they had taken a break for lunch, so much of what they were talking about was hypothetical and that drained them. Until there was a 'live' project to work on, neither would be able to judge how much information Debbie had retained.

"I think my brain's about to explode," joked Debbie.

"Mine too," said Jenny, "shall we call it a day?" Debbie agreed and closed her notepad. She packed away the rest of her things plus the folders Jenny had given her to read. Jenny offered Debbie a cup of tea, but she said no as she had to be off shortly because she was due to collect her son from the nursery.

"Phew," thought Jenny as she slumped onto the sofa after seeing Debbie out. She looked up at the clock on the wall and realized it was almost time for her to collect her own children from school.

The next day was the conference Jenny had been looking forward to. She hadn't been to anything like this before and wasn't sure what to expect. Simon was occasionally asked to speak at conferences and she helped him to practice what he was going to say.

She collected her name badge in the entrance hall and when the conference was about to start she took her seat. Looking around her she estimated there were somewhere between 150 and 200 women business owners. It was quite exciting, she thought. She smiled at the person next to her and introduced herself. Going to the exhibition some weeks ago when she spoke to the Duty Manager of the hotel and got ideas, gave her confidence to talk to the people around her now.

The compère took to the stage and introduced the first speaker, a female entrepreneur who had started her own children's clothing business from home and which flourished after she started selling on the internet. It was an inspirational talk full of ideas, yet she couldn't really grasp how selling online could work for a business like hers.

The second speaker, an internet marketing expert, talked about using keywords on your website and how to advertise online. After the first five minutes she was feeling lost and out of her depth. It seemed as if everyone else understood what she was talking about and was making lots of notes. Jenny considered herself pretty computer savvy, but this was an area she simply wasn't familiar with.

The final speaker before lunch took to the stage. She put a slide up which simply read 'The Tuna Curry Story'. Jenny was intrigued and it took a few minutes of introductory speaking, before she started the story:

"The tuna curry story dates back to when I was a poor student. If you've been a student, you'll identify with this. It was one of those days when the cupboards are looking bare and you have to get 'creative' with what you've got left. I reached into the cupboard and found a packet of curry powder. 'I know,' I thought, 'I'll make a curry. Now, what do you usually put in a curry? Meat,' I thought. I opened the fridge looking for meat, but didn't find any. I looked in the cupboard again and found a tin of tuna in brine. 'That'll do,' I thought. 'Okay, what else goes in a curry?' I usually ate chicken korma, so thought 'cream or yogurt'. In the fridge I'd seen one of those yogurts with the fruit in a separate pot on the side, so I reached for that. I didn't use the strawberry part, I might add! I poured the curry powder, tuna in brine and yogurt into the saucepan, put the gas on and stirred."

The audience winced and looked horrified. "As you've probably guessed, the smell was disgusting. The yogurt began to curdle in the salt water. I took one mouthful and knew instantly I'd made a terrible mistake. The taste it left in my mouth was awful! Of course, after making such a bad mistake, I might have been tempted to give up on cooking altogether, but thankfully I've persevered and learned how to do it myself now. With hindsight what I should have done was get a recipe book or speak to someone who actually knew what they were doing." She paused for effect.

"How often do we do this in business? We try to make things up as we go along and wonder why it doesn't turn out perfectly first time. There's very little which is new in the business world and that's a good thing because it means whatever you're currently trying to do in your business, someone else has done it before. And those who have done it well know the recipe for success you're looking for. Unless you're happy for your business to end up like a tuna curry, it's okay to ask for help and go to people who know about how to do something than you do. The idea of 'fake it til you make it' is often talked about in small businesses and is valid up until a point. That point is where pretending you know everything there is to know stops you from getting advice in time because you don't want to lose face, feel embarrassed or even not be able to take 100% credit for the success of your business."

Jenny was stunned. The speaker had a fairly direct way of talking, but it made her reconsider her decision not to ask her mum for any more advice. She began to make notes of her own.

The speaker now put up a slide of a well-stocked larder and continued her presentation. "Have you ever been in the situation where someone says to you 'there's nothing to eat' and you go into the cupboard and see something like this? I'm sure there are plenty of you who would take one look and say, 'for goodness sake, there are loads of things to eat' and you'd be able to create a lovely meal from the ingredients you see in front of you. There will be others among you who struggle to put together a meal unless it's ready-made or tells you how to prepare it on the label. The well-stocked larder is a bit like the internet. It's full of information and possibilities - provided you know how to put all the various ingredients together."

"Let's say you want to know how to build your business through marketing. You look on the shelves, i.e. online, and see sites about different marketing techniques such as advertising, PR, email marketing, social media, direct mail and various other ingredients. Different people have different preferences for food. Some will tell you social media is the best thing since sliced bread and is the only way to go. Others whose customers have different tastes will tell you offline direct mail is best. There are some people who dislike certain techniques and avoid using them as much as someone with a nut allergy avoids nuts. Of course, you can eat individual ingredients individually but they work best in combination with others. That's why an integrated campaign which brings together various ingredients communicating a similar message tends to be more effective. It's no good to try social media on its own for a few months until your customers are sick of seeing you there, then suddenly switch all your activity to direct mail and bombard them with letters and brochures, then when you fail to get results, say neither ingredient works."

"To create an appetizing dish, use ingredients which work together in the right proportions. If you know what you're doing that's great. If you're not sure, use a recipe book or ask an expert 'chef' for help. You don't have to make it all up yourself. Some food for thought, eh?" The audience nodded. She concluded her talk and explained that if people wanted help working out their particular recipe for success and making it all happen, her company could help.

The compère thanked her for her talk and announced that it was time for lunch. Rather than rushing out to be first in line for the buffet, Jenny decided instead to sit and ponder what she had just heard. "I'm at that point in my own business where I'm getting overwhelmed by all the information out there," she thought. "I have someone who I could go to for help, but for some reason I've not done it as often as I should. I wonder why that is."

~

"Hi Sasha, come on in," Simon said. He'd changed the venue for their coaching session this time and met at the members club he belonged to. He liked it there and felt at ease, plus it meant they were away from the distractions at the office. Sasha had said a few times it would be better for them to meet off-site and until today he hadn't really appreciated the benefits of doing so. He'd thought he'd be saving time if she came to his office, yet knowing he needed to be somewhere at a certain time meant he finished his previous meetings promptly where previously he might have let them run over and kept her waiting a few minutes. Also he was able to use the travelling time to think and plan for their session and would be able to go straight home afterwards. They walked together to the meeting room he'd booked and chatted on the way.

Sasha sat down and took out her notes from their last meeting. "So Simon, how have things been since we last met?" He explained about Andy and Rebekah working better together, how Karen was being included in discussions and the presentation from the agency.

"Things are going really well and it's weird that I actually feel more in control by letting other people take ownership of things and letting them run projects. I don't need to micro manage so much or stand over their shoulder whispering about budgets! You were right," he added, "I do have a resourceful team of people around me. I count myself very lucky."

"You know what Simon?" said Sasha. "One of characteristics I've seen in the best leaders is they hire people much smarter than themselves. It might be a strange thing to say, but if you know other people can do things better than you can it's very freeing, as you've experienced. You don't feel the pressure to do everything yourself and to know everything. It's also incredibly empowering for the people who work for you because they know you trust and respect them. In contrast the worst leaders and the ones who only hire people they can dominate, both intellectually and emotionally. They push away their best people and destroy the confidence of everyone who's left. They are the ones who you'll hear complaining and saying, "You just can't find good staff these days" or words to that effect. All credit to you that you're recognizing what people are good at and letting your people shine."

Simon kept a straight face while inside he was beaming and jumping for joy. "Thanks Sasha, that's good to know." His face cracked and he did allow himself a smile.

"Simon, in your email you said there were a couple of things you wanted to work on today: internal communications and leadership skills. Could you flesh that out a bit so we've got something specific to work towards? Each of those topics could fill a five-day course." They talked and narrowed down their focus to be how to let the rest of the staff know about what was happening with the launch of the new courses, in particular the goal for the coaching session would be to write a draft plan for the internal communications. "Great, thanks Simon, that's something we can work on in the next hour and a half."

He explained about the cooking analogies which kept cropping up and how he'd like to try to incorporate them into the communications. "Everyone eats and pretty much everyone has cooked a meal, so it's something that goes across departments and levels of seniority. It also means people don't need an academic business background or know all the jargon to understand what we're getting at." He told her how powerful Rebekah's message about marketing needing time to cook had been. He also told her about Jenny's mum's dinner party analogies, how useful Jenny had found them and what a difference it had made to her business. "I suppose what I'd like to do is show everyone how they have a part to play in cooking a meal, but that doesn't usually happen in a kitchen."

"It does if you're running a restaurant," Sasha pointed out, "You have the head chef running the kitchen and specialists in each kind of dish. You also have the front of house staff and all the waiting staff. You need a process for taking orders, prioritizing them and getting the kitchen to prepare them so each table gets their course all served together and they're not waiting for someone to get their food while everyone else's goes cold."

"Yes! The new courses are literally new courses on the menu! I love it!" He started frantically writing notes on everything they'd just discussed. Throughout the rest of the session they found themselves coming up with cooking puns and analogies. He had so many ideas and was eager to tell someone about them so when they had finished, he couldn't wait to get home and talk it over with Jenny.

As he drove home he reflected on how useful it was to have thinking time immediately after the session. When he and Sasha had met in his office, he found that Angela had often booked another meeting soon after so he didn't get a chance to really process and plan his next steps. He made a mental note to ask Angela not to book any other meetings on afternoons when he had coaching sessions. He really wanted to make sure he made the most of it and it would mean a better return on investment for the company. It wasn't helping the company if his recollections of coaching sessions were sketchy because he hadn't given himself time to think. His mind was made up. He'd speak to Angela in the morning.

He arrived home an hour earlier than he would normally, having missed most of the traffic. "Simon, is that you?" Jenny called from bathroom. He could hear the splashing and squeals of children playing in the bath. He shook off his jacket, left his case at the door and bounded up the stairs.

"Daddy!" the children called out as he poked his head around the open bathroom door. They held up their arms for a cuddle. It was a split-second decision, get wet or miss cuddles. He opted for getting wet.

"You're early," said Jenny as she leaned in to kiss Simon.

"Yep, I had a meeting with my coach and decided to come straight home afterwards. There wasn't any point going back to the office - and I would have missed bath time!" he looked at his children and started splashing the water playfully. The screeches of delight were ear-piercing.

They splashed back a bit more water than he'd expected - more like a tidal wave as they stood up in the bath and started kicking water around - and he was glad he wasn't wearing anything expensive. Jenny was relieved she'd put the anti-slip bathmats securely in place before filling the tub. "Come on you lot, time for fluffy cuddles!" said Jenny as she passed a big bath towel to Simon and said, "One each?" They wrapped each child in a fluffy towel and cuddled and tickled them to dry them off. It was the only way Jenny had found to make them keen to get out of the bath. Her old phrase 'time to get out' never went down very well.

They each lifted one up and carried them into the bedroom.

"Thank you," Jenny mouthed to Simon over her shoulder. Excited that Daddy was home early, neither child was particularly eager to get changed into their pajamas, knowing it was a sign bedtime was coming, so there was a lot of running around and bouncing on beds. It was alright because they had made up a lot of time with Simon helping dry them off.

They played some games together, including 'who can get in their jim jams quickest?' and as Simon started counting 1...2....3.... they leapt into action and were shouting 'I win' within seconds. "Well done both of you - that was *fantastic*! I don't think I've ever seen anyone get in their jim jams that fast! I think you've both earned an extra special story tonight. Who wants to hear it?"

"Me, me!" Rosie and Noah said excitedly and each jumped onto their beds.

"Okay well you'd better get snuggled up so I can tell you it because it's a very special story indeed. You won't find it any books because it's too special for other children to know." This kind of talk always got them intrigued; they loved to hear how they were special.

Jenny slipped out of the room mouthing, "I'll leave you to it. I'll be in the kitchen," and Simon nodded as he got ready to tell his story.

"Once upon a time there was a special little girl called Rosie and a special little boy called Noah...." Their favorite stories were the ones where they were the main characters and were mesmerized. They didn't even mind too much that they were called 'little' in the story. "Silly Daddy. We're big now" Rosie whispered to Noah.

As the story drew to a close Rosie had already shut her eyes and Noah's head started nodding as he desperately tried to stay awake long enough to hear what happened. He was fighting a losing battle and his tiredness got the better of him.

Simon kissed each of their foreheads, turned the lighting down and crept out of the room. He then started his ninja-performance as he tried to dodge the creaky boards on the stairs. He could hear Jenny in the kitchen as he descended.

"Thank you so much darling," she said. "The kids loved it that you were home early". She put down the tea towel she was holding and put her arms around his neck, "and I loved it too." He held her round her waist and kissed her. "So how was your day?" Jenny asked, "You had a coaching session, right?"

"Yeah, good. I'm getting a lot out of it." He gazed into her eyes, "you know when Karen first suggested it, I wasn't sure, but I can see it's beneficial to take time and step back from things." He told her about the events of the day and how he was planning to use the cooking analogies to get the message across to staff about what needed to be done. Jenny laughed and told him about the conference. She agreed it was a good idea and they brainstormed more cooking themes and phrases as Simon's dinner reheated in the microwave, a conversation they continued when he took his food through to the lounge.

Later in the evening when they went to bed, Simon noticed how much more relaxed he felt - more so than he had for weeks. He had a clear plan in mind for the company, he'd been able to spend time with his family and Jenny was happier and more affectionate.

Sasha was right, letting other people take ownership meant he wasn't feeling the weight of the world on his shoulders. He began to feel like he was part of a team at work. He didn't usually think of himself as a team player, even though everyone always says they are on their CV. When his head hit the pillow he drifted off into a deep, restful sleep.

The next morning over breakfast Simon watched the news reports about another storm heading their way and didn't pay much attention to it other than choose his waterproof jacket from the hook in the hallway.

Simon took his time driving to the office and arrived refreshed having taken the scenic route away from the main roads. When he arrived Angela greeted him, "Good morning! You're popular already."

"Morning Angela. What do you mean about being popular?" asked Simon.

"Karen and Andy have already been asking for time in your diary today. You're seeing Karen first at 10, hope that's okay."

"Yes, that's okay; there are some things I wanted to talk over with her anyway." He continued into his office and opened up his email inbox after hanging his coat on the hook. Angela followed him in with some notes to go through and they sat at the table in Simon's office. He explained about the need to keep his diary clear after coaching sessions and she agreed to do that. She seemed very organized today and funnily enough, so did he. He liked it when Angela took the initiative and managed upwards, telling him where he needed to be and when, who he needed to talk to, what about and briefed him on what else was going on in the office, including any whispers she'd heard. "I see Andy and Rebekah are getting along better now. It's really having a positive impact on the other people around them. The tension had been unbearable," Angela offered, secretly hoping for some extra morsel of information. She couldn't help herself. Normally she was very discrete and didn't pry but she really wanted to know what was going on. There was a buzz around the office these days and she wanted to be a part of it.

"Yes, it's good isn't it? This training project seems to be bringing all the different functions together. I really must bring you up to speed now it's all been agreed," said Simon.

"You've got a gap in your diary at two, could we catch up then?"

"Good idea," said Simon. "I'll see you at two. All done for now?" Angela nodded and Simon pushed his chair back to get up from the table and turned to his desk. She left him to continue catching up on messages.

Simon checked through his emails, making a note of what he needed to get done that day. For all that they were a company selling and promoting technology he always found it easier to write out his 'to do' list by hand each day. There was something very satisfying about crossing items off. It wasn't quite the same when they simply disappeared from a task list on a screen. Before he knew it an automated reminder pinged on his screen telling him his meeting with Karen would be in five minutes. "Angela must have set that up when she put it in my diary," he thought. "She's so organized," and he smiled to himself.

Sure enough at 10am Karen knocked and came in. Unusually she shut the door behind her. "Must be serious," he joked.

"No, not serious," she said. "Just private. I'm conscious Angela can hear everything being so close to the door."

"Fair enough. Who's in trouble?" asked Simon.

"No one's in trouble. In fact I wanted to catch up with you and find out how the coaching is going."

"Oh, right. I haven't spoken to you about that since I started with Sasha, have I? It's going great. I was saying to my wife last night that when you first suggested it I wasn't sure, but I'm finding it very useful."

"I'm pleased to hear that! I got the impression things were going well. And," she paused for effect, "I have to say people are starting to notice a difference."

Simon leaned in. He wanted to hear more and at the same time wanted to appear nonchalant about it. He put his elbow on the table, rested his head on his open hand and looked curious, "Oh? What's been said?"

"Okay, I'm not naming names, but apparently that day Andy had his outburst, it made a lot of people nervous. When you both left the office together, people expected fireworks, so they were really surprised when you came back appearing to be best buddies. What happened?" she gave the impression that she was genuinely interested.

"That was a few weeks back, let me think. We just talked things over and sorted it out." He struggled to remember the details of what had happened because so much had moved on since then.

"Oh come on Simon, this is me you're talking to. You can tell me. What happened?" Karen had obviously mistaken his poor recollections for being evasive, so he tried harder to recall the conversation.

"I decided to listen to what he was saying. He told me his thoughts about running courses, which I thought sounded like a good idea and said so."

"Is that it?" Karen sounded surprised.

"In a nutshell, yes."

"And what's the deal with Rebekah and Andy burying the hatchet? Things have really improved there."

"I suppose it's the same kind of thing. Listening and trying to understand what's going on. I had a one-to-one with Rebekah and asked her about what she needed. Oh yes! I remember now! I used an old coaching 'mind trick'," he moved his hands about and wiggled his fingers. This went down better than the 'shoot' action he'd used with Rebekah and Karen smiled. He was relieved. "Sasha told me about something called the GROW model, let me see if I can remember. You get them to tell you the Goal – that's what they're trying to achieve. Then it's the Reality – what's going on, what they've done so far and that kind of thing. Now, what's the O...?"

"Options," Karen added.

"You know it?" asked Simon.

"Yes," she filled in the gaps for him. "It's Goal, Reality, Options and Way forward or what they Will do. I trained as a coach, remember?"

"Ah, I'd forgotten that. Yes, you're right about GROW. So I used that with her and it worked a treat. I got her to come up with her own ideas on how she could get what she needed from Andy. I could have told her what I thought she should do, which was just go and ask him, but the ideas she came up with actually ended up leading to a better solution. It's hard trying to shut up and listen sometimes isn't it?"

"But worth it if you can bite your tongue and let them come up with solutions," said Karen.

"Indeed. I think her attitude towards him changed after that."

Karen put down the pen she was holding. "Simon, I've been very impressed with how you've taken to coaching. Do you remember you asked me about getting a motivational speaker in?"

"Oh yes, I did, didn't I?" He realized just how much the situation had altered in the space of a few weeks.

"I don't think you need to. Your new approach is working and people are motivating themselves."

"Do you think so?" Simon wasn't used to receiving positive feedback outside of an appraisal and he felt a little uncomfortable.

"Yes, I seriously do. Do you also remember we talked about you having coaching first and then maybe offering it to the directors? So it cascades down?" He nodded a few times enthusiastically. "Well," she continued, "some of them have already taken the initiative. I've been asked confidentially by two people if they can have some of what you're having!"

"Is that a good thing?" he asked innocently.

"A very good thing. It doesn't usually happen this fast so you must be making an impression."

"What's the next step then? I assume there's an allowance in the budget for this?" he asked.

"When we had the initial discussion, I made sure we had enough in there, so I'll get on and organize things if that's okay with you?" Karen asked.

"Just one request. Sasha's great. I'd like to keep her as *my* coach. Could you find other people for the directors?"

"If you're worried about confidentiality, Sasha's very professional..." Karen's voice tailed off and Simon jumped in with his comments.

"I'd just feel better if the directors have someone else." Simon was firm.

Karen tried to persuade and reassure him what was discussed in sessions was confidential and Sasha wouldn't even hint at anything that had been said behind closed doors, but Simon's mind appeared to be made up. She had other options. Sasha worked closely with other coaches and could recommend people now she had a better understanding of the culture and the situation. The good thing, she reflected, was the coaching was having an impact and people wanted it.

Simon's next meeting was with the directors plus Rebekah, so Karen stayed in his office while the others started to assemble. The meeting was to discuss the courses, who needed to do what and to fine tune deadlines for completion. Other than chairing the meeting, Simon found he didn't need to get too involved because they had all come well-prepared.

Once there was agreement on which departments would be taking charge of each area, the discussion turned to internal communications. Simon explained his thoughts on using the cooking analogies and acknowledged Rebekah's contributions on this. He suggested a meeting for all of the staff so he could tell everyone what was happening. Some of the directors looked down and shifted in their chairs. He couldn't put his finger on what had caused the change in tone of the meeting and then it finally struck him; *they* wanted to be involved in giving the presentation. He changed tack and suggested making the opening speech and then bringing each of them in to present their area. This got their attention and they re-engaged in the meeting.

The sandwiches arrived and Angela brought them through into the office. It had become something of a tradition to have a working lunch during these meetings.

The conversations continued for some time and it was eventually agreed the staff meeting would happen next Monday morning and each person would present a five minute overview of their area. The only person who wasn't keen to present was Diane, the Finance Director. Simon accepted this without question and if he was being honest with himself, he wasn't really sure whether presenting the costs of the project was the best way forward. It would be better for the numbers to come from Andy.

After the meeting, Simon reflected that it was a bold move to be so open about the sales targets for the course. Until recently each sales person had their own targets, but many didn't know what the overall numbers were. Certainly the other departments didn't seem to have any idea about the targets – and how they were falling short of them. As he thought about it, he started getting nervous and began wondering if he had made an error of judgment.

Simon looked at his watch. He had 25 minutes before he was due to meet with Angela and he needed time to clear his head. In a way this would be a rehearsal of Monday's presentation. He looked out of the window and the rain was coming down hard. Grabbing his coat from the back of his office door, he ventured out into the wet weather, heading for the coffee shop across the road.

With only a few minutes to go before his meeting with Angela, Simon walked back into the office. "It's bucketing down out there," he said as he passed Angela's desk removing his rain-soaked coat. "Give me five and I'll be ready."

Sure enough, five minutes later Angela poked her head around the door and continued into his office.

Simon took time to explain what was happening, the reasons for it and how it would all work. He hesitated before discussing the numbers, but then accepted that Angela had access to confidential information like this anyway and could be trusted.

He was surprised by her reaction.

When he told her the targets she was thoughtful. She asked some insightful questions about how achievable the targets were, how much marketing would be happening and who would be on-site to up-sell to the clients attending the courses. Perhaps he had misjudged her. "Angela, how do you think the staff will react to what we're about to present to them?" he asked.

She paused before replying and finally said, "I think it'll go down very well. There's been a lot of gossip recently, especially when you joined and a lot of fears about the changes you might bring in. This will give people confidence that the company has a future and help them see the part they can play in it. You might get two or three skeptics. You can't worry about them too much. They're just moaners who'll say this isn't on their job description – I could probably tell you now who they'll be!"

"What about the numbers?" Simon asked. He started to realize the main reason he hadn't been comfortable being open about the numbers was that he knew there hadn't been any pay raises in a while and he was worried there would be a backlash when staff realized the company did have money to spend. He was dreading the question: so why don't we carry on doing what we know how to do and put the money into our salaries? As he pondered this, he came to the realization that if anyone highlighted this as a problem it would be Karen, and yet she hadn't mentioned it at all. Was he being paranoid? He then justified it to himself that the numbers should be kept secret in case competitors found out about them.

"...and I think that'll be okay if you present it positively. Are you going to do that or is Andy?" Angela looked at him expectantly.

Simon was embarrassed and jolted himself back into the moment. He hadn't been listening and had no idea what Angela was saying. "Sorry, my mind was off thinking through something you'd said earlier. Could you run that past me again?" Fortunately Angela didn't take offence and was happy to repeat what she had just said.

The following Monday was the big day. Unusually all members of staff were on time and some were even early. They assembled in the conference room on the second floor of the building. Simon walked along the central aisle to the front and a hush followed him. He could feel the tension in the air. The faces in the audience looked concerned: were they going to be made redundant? Had the company been sold? Had they lost a major contract? Simon knew he needed to address those concerns early on otherwise people wouldn't pay attention until he did.

After being introduced by Andy, Simon opened proceedings. "Thank you everyone for your attention today. This meeting will take about 45 minutes. I know many of you have questions about the future which you want to have answered. I also know that most of you are very busy and will be eager to get back to your desks after we finish, so may I ask that we hold questions until the end? We have allowed time to answer as many of them as possible."

Simon went on to explain the current trading position, the research Andy and his team had been conducting with Rebekah and the outcome, which was to launch a new line of training products. This seemed to allay people's fears. He introduced the first presentation from his team, took his seat at the front and looked out into the audience. Angela had been right. The three people she'd said would be the skeptics were each alternating between whispering to the people next to them and sitting back in their chairs, arms crossed and scowling. He'd handle them separately. He knew he'd need to make sure their skepticism was handled positively and while Andy was delivering his part of the presentation, Simon had a brainwave. He remembered reading in one of the books Sasha had suggested to him something about team roles. Was it Belbin or something like that? He tried to remember. The gist of it was that in order for teams to be effective there needs to be a mix of personalities taking different roles. One of the important roles was to bring people back down to earth and make sure all flaws in a plan were minimized. Aha! He'd found a job for the skeptics! While the others were presenting, he mentally made a note and started rehearsing in his mind how he would present this to them.

When it was time for him to present his conclusion and open the floor to questions, he was ready. "Thank you all for listening. I'm sure you have lots of questions. Some of you may have valid points about how this can work even better. I want you all to know that as a management team, we want to hear from you. All I ask is that if you have points to raise about anything we've missed or something you think hasn't been considered but should be, when you come to us you bring us solutions, instead of problems. Everyone has a part to play in making this successful. You're the people on the ground who know more about the day-to-day running of the business than we do, so we rely on you to quickly spot when something can be done better. While we can't promise you'll get everything you ask for, we do promise to listen and consider what you say." He saw two of the skeptics reach for their notepads and start writing. The third cocked their head. "Who would like to open with the first question?" Simon asked.

People looked around at each other, waiting to see who would be the first. Nothing. Eventually, the skeptic who had been sat at the front unfolded their arms raised his hand and spoke, "I'm Nigel the Technical Support Manager. My team is already working at full capacity. It's good that the users are going to be trained on the advanced features of the software, but after the training course ends, they'll be coming back to us for help. We can turn around the easy requests quickly, but handling more advanced problems is going to take longer. We could end up hugely under-resourced. What is the company going to do about this?"

"Thank you so much Nigel and nice to meet you," said Simon. "I don't think there are many people in this business who know as much about the kinds of questions you get asked as your team and how you schedule your work. Tell you what, if you can prepare some suggestions for handling this, let's have a meeting next week to go through them. Does that work for you?" Nigel said yes and Simon turned to Angela, "Could you arrange a time for a meeting with Nigel please?" Simon thought to himself that he already knew what Nigel would come up with as the solution: more staff. Angela had the exact same thought.

Throughout the week, there was a positive mood in the office. Angela made a suggestion to Simon that they open a 'solutions box' in the office. This would be like a suggestions box, with the emphasis squarely on solutions. Simon thought it was worth a try and let Angela handle the email to all staff letting them know about it. The box was placed in the staff kitchen so notes could be slipped into it discretely.

At the end of the third day Angela collected the box and took it to her desk. She was curious to find out what people had written. There were a couple of sarcastic comments. Her heart sank as she read them. She felt annoyed and embarrassed that something she'd thought would be a positive move had backfired. She wasn't sure whether or not to tell Simon.

While she was mulling it over Andy walked up to her desk carrying an open envelope. "Hi Angie," he said. "I've got something for the suggestions box but it wasn't in the kitchen. Is Simon around?"

"He's seeing someone in the meeting room and isn't due out for about an hour. Do you want to leave that with me?" she asked.

"Okay, but I think this needs actioning as soon as possible," he said as Angela took the envelope from him. "Sanjay has written up his thoughts on how we can improve the on-site presence at the training courses and up-sell other products. It's very good and I'd like to see that he gets credit for it. He brought it to me before putting it in the box." He paused before continuing, "I'm going to go ahead with it and brief the sales team straight away. I wondered if there was something we could do to show that we're taking people's comments on board."

Angela felt elated. After her initial disappointment over the sarcastic comments, here was an example of her idea actually working. "Leave it with me Andy and I'll make sure he knows about it today. Maybe we could send out a follow-up email to everyone once all your team know about it. It might encourage other people to come forward with ideas." She sat back in her chair and smiled.   Today was a good day.

Recipe for a United Workforce

'Our people are our greatest asset': Perhaps the most over-used phrase in business, but it demonstrates just how many organizations recognize that without the right people on board working together towards a common aim they are unlikely to succeed.

The most effective workforces acknowledge the contribution made by each individual and binds them together with a sense of shared purpose.

Not unlike a chocolate chip cookie.

Creating the perfect chocolate chip cookie is actually quite a straightforward process. This recipe shows you how to make a cookie which is crispy on the outside and chewy on this inside.

Ingredients
Flour, bicarbonate of soda, salt, butter, caster sugar, brown sugar, vanilla extract, eggs, chocolate chips

Preparation
Wash your hands – regardless of what has gone before, creating a united workforce means wiping the slate clean and starting fresh. It may take a while to wash away thoughts of office politics, mergers, redundancies and difficult staff, so using a detergent can help.

This detergent can take the form of consulting key representatives from all levels of the organization that have a vested interest in creating a united workforce and putting the past behind them. The cleansing process will take time as it's about healing old wounds and changing attitudes. The more support you have from all ranks the easier it will be to spot dissent amongst the staff and deal with it before it spreads. Equally, just as detergent in washing up water pushes aside grease and fat, some people may decide it's time for them to move on from the organization. This is a natural part of the process and is to be expected where certain individuals have a personal interest in maintaining the status quo and are unwilling or unable to change.

Method
Pre-heat the oven – when you decide to work on uniting your workforce, give people some notice that things are going to look and feel different. The same people who have helped you to wash your hands can now begin to spread the word that things are starting to warm up. While you prepare the dough for the cookies, the oven needs to get up to temperature. Many people find change scary, so let them get used to the changes that are coming gradually.

In a bowl, combine the butter, sugar, brown sugar and vanilla extract until creamy - having consulted with key members of staff when washing your hands, the senior management at the heart of creating your cookie need time to combine their thoughts and ideas. They need to be fully aligned before introducing new ingredients into the mix. This stage is where the sweetness is added to the cookie, so focus on all the positive points about the changes you and your team are planning to make and how they will benefit everyone. When the ingredients are fully combined, there should be absolute agreement on what kind of cookie you're all trying to make.

In another bowl combine the flour, bicarbonate of soda and salt – this stage is about getting the HR side of things organized. For example, policies and procedures may need to be updated, staff handbooks and recruitment processes will most likely need to be reviewed and there needs to a clear process for managing people out of the business if they are unwilling to co-operate.

First beat in the eggs, then gradually beat in the flour mixture – just as the eggs bind the mixture together and add moisture before the dry ingredients are added, your senior team may need to get used to the idea of bringing in the procedural side of the changes. Without the eggs' moisture, the mix can become very dry and difficult to blend. Even with it, significant effort may need to go into making the mixture bind together.

Gently stir in the chocolate chips – in order to preserve the individuality of each member of your staff, they need to be handled with care. Try beating them into the mix and you risk losing everything about them which adds value to the organization. The best organizations blend different personalities into a whole while giving everyone a voice.

Spoon the mixture onto a baking tray leaving space around each cookie for them to spread and bake in the oven – as your people settle into the new way of doing things, they need space to expand and to grow on a personal and professional level. While it may be tempting to cram too many cookies onto the baking tray, during the process of cooking they will overlap each other and get in each other's way. Ensure that your processes and ways of doing things allow people to make their own decisions and think for themselves rather than being tied up in 'red tape'.

When cooked, remove from the oven and place on a wire tray to cool before eating – when creating a united workforce, your people need to keep their shape in all situations – whether they are in a fast-paced 'hot' period or a slower 'cooler' period. Allow them time to adapt to this change.

Enjoy!

FOOD FOR THOUGHT...

EI / EQ / NLP – What are they?

It used to be that the only qualification you needed to successfully manage people and interact with customers was seniority. The more years you had under belt doing a particular job, the thinking went, the better able you were to handle the extra responsibilities and challenges of being "in charge".

The world of business has changed dramatically since those days, and so have the qualifications you need to be successful.

Research shows that entrepreneurs tend to have a high level of technical skills in whatever field their business operates in. This is a real advantage when getting a business off the ground, but as the business grows and matures an entirely different and new set of skills is required to create long term success. These are sometimes called 'soft skills', and they are much more focused on non-technical things that may seem unimportant at first but are actually critical to the survival and prosperity of your business. If you are not actively developing your soft skills, you are operating at a distinct disadvantage in today's business environment.

To lead and manage staff effectively, to build good working relationships with suppliers, and to continue winning the business of both new and existing customers, you must be able to relate to people. This is not just about knowing how to make small talk and be polite; rather, it is about being able to "read" people, empathize with their feelings, and customize your interactions so that you can best meet their individual needs.

There are three popular descriptions and approaches related to the soft skills that are so incredibly important:

Emotional Intelligence (EI)
This is the concept that revolves around your capacity and ability to identify, evaluate, and manage your own emotions and those of others.

Emotional Intelligence Quotient (EQ)
This is the measurement that quantifies your levels of EI; it is a relatively new measurement and as such can vary widely in acceptance and understanding.

Neuro-Linguistic Programming (NLP)
This is the concept that models interpersonal communications by combining the impacts and effects of both behavior patterns and the subjective experiences you have while demonstrating those behavior patterns.

It used to be that these were simply known as social skills, but we now know they go much deeper and have a much greater influence on success than ever thought before. The increasing role of the internet in our lives, including the dramatic rise of social networking sites such as LinkedIn.com, Facebook and Twitter means 'business as usual' no longer exists.

If you want to prosper and succeed, you must continuously develop and strengthen these kinds of skills because they give you the ability to interact with others in a way that is mutually beneficial and rewarding.

FIND OUT MORE...
For more tips, tools and resources go to:
www.businesscookerybook.com/resources

Chapter 9

"Hi Jenny. How's the weather over there? I've been hearing on the news that you've had some pretty bad storms," said Barbara.

"Yes, it's been bad. The rain's been very heavy," said Jenny. "Luckily we're up on the hill so we're not at risk of flooding, but the next town's in a valley and the river broke its banks last year. I hope it doesn't happen again."

"You said in your email you wanted to talk more about the publicity for your work at the hotel," said Barbara. "I've been having a think about it and I've had some ideas."

"That would be fantastic Mum. And Mum, I'm sorry for not asking for your help sooner. I suppose I was being a bit big-headed and wanted to do it all myself," admitted Jenny.

"Well, you've been like it all your life, you're not going to change now," said Barbara.

"Oi!" said Jenny.

"I meant you're independent and you don't really rely on anyone else," explained Barbara quickly. "It's a good trait to have in business because you take responsibility for things. I should know, I was always very much the 'take charge' person in the business your Dad and I ran together. The downside is you can take on too much and overload yourself. You've got the kids to consider as well. When we launched our agency you and Susie were already in college, so things were different for us." Susie was Jenny's older sister.

"I'd forgotten that," said Jenny. "Mum I've never really told you this but I always admired you and Dad for the business you built. This is going to sound crazy, but I was trying to measure up to you. I wanted to prove to you both and also to me that I could do it on my own."

"Jenny, that's a lovely thing to know, but I think you might not know the full story of how we built the business to the size we did." Barbara wondered whether she should tell Jenny about the sacrifices she and her husband had made. She decided her daughter ought to know. "We didn't talk to you or your sister about the ins and outs of the business, because, well, we wanted to shield you from the big financial risk we were taking. We had to re-mortgage the house at one point and I had to beg my mum - your Gran - to give us a big loan." Barbara paused. "Do you remember how the back room was always full of boxes and you weren't allowed to touch them?"

"Yes," Jenny laughed, "I do remember that now."

"That's because I'd taken a home-working job packing tights!" Barbara laughed as well. "Yes, tights! I was terrified you or Susie would either snag them or pinch them to wear on a night out. The money was terrible but it meant I could get paid and still be able to answer the phone if any potential clients called for the agency. Your Dad was out all day doing the rounds of all the people he used to work with to get business. The first few projects he did for next to nothing to build his portfolio and get testimonials from clients. In those days people really took advantage because times were tough and they knew we needed the work." As Barbara recalled those dark times, she felt the emotion of it all over again. "One client took over six months to pay his bill and another client took all John's ideas and appointed another agency to do the work. Nine months of work setting up the deal went down the drain. All the time you were in art college we were living off borrowed money. It took over three years before we could start paying any of it back." She paused before telling Jenny the full story. "You might remember Gran being very grumpy whenever we visited her. That's because we used to have furious arguments over the loan. Eventually she told us she'd given up on ever getting it back and she'd write it off as my inheritance and take me out of her will. When she had her stroke a year later, the rest of the family blamed me and your Dad and shut us out." Jenny could hear her mum's voice tremble and grow quieter.

"I had no idea Mum," Jenny whispered. There was silence on the line and Jenny could just about make out sniffing sounds.

Eventually Barbara spoke, "Jenny, there's no way I EVER want you to be in that situation. Forget trying to live up to any expectations you think we have of you. We are already SO proud of you my darling."

Jenny felt tears welling up in her eyes and a knot in her throat.

"Darling, I want to help you," Barbara assured her. "The one thing I learned how to do when we had no money was how to get PR. It doesn't cost you anything and I'm being deadly serious when I say that when we started doing it, the business turned around within a year and we were making good money. By that stage the damage was done, but at least in the last two years of Gran's life we could afford to put her in a decent nursing home."

Jenny now remembered her Mum going to see her Gran every week and sometimes going with her. On one occasion she remembered Gran shouting at her calling her a money-grabber and accusing her of trying to kill her by poisoning her tea so she wouldn't have to pay for the home. Jenny had put it down to dementia brought on by her stroke. At the time it had made her Mum cry terribly and she had comforted her. She now realized what had been going on behind closed doors.

"Mum, I would be honored if you would help me. In fact I'd be really proud if you did," Jenny said.

Barbara blew her nose and Jenny could hear that she was composing herself. "Right, okay, let's get started. You want to get in the national glossy furnishing magazines, don't you? If you start now, I can show you how to get coverage for the February editions – they are the ones published in the New Year. I'll also show you how to get in the specialist magazines and the regional magazines and newspapers. It's going to take some work and you're going to have to be ballsy, but if you do what I tell you, your business is going to do very well out of it. Are you prepared to put in the work and do things that might be outside of what you're normally comfortable with?"

"Absolutely. I can't afford the luxury of only doing the things that are easy. Mum, if you've got the recipe for this and you'll show me how to do it, I'd be mad to say no!"

Jenny put her faith in her mum and did exactly what she had been told to do. She surprised herself and once she started contacting the media, it was easier than she imagined. She'd expected to be met with dismissive journalists, but by doing what her mum told her to do, she got interest from several of them.

With Debbie's help, she managed to get enough interest from the regional media to put on a re-launch event at Derek's hotel and the following week the regional newspaper ran a feature on it with photos showing the quirkier rooms.

Jenny's phone rang. "Jenny, it's Derek, can you talk?"

"Sure," she said.

"Things are going crazy down here," he sounded agitated. "Since the story ran in the paper, we've been inundated with calls from people wanting to book functions and rooms."

"That's great – and that's what you wanted wasn't it?" Jenny was puzzled.

"It would be if the function room wasn't under a foot of water!" She could hear the panic in his voice and suddenly realized what had happened - the storms! The hotel was in a picturesque location overlooking the river in the valley and the function room was on the side facing the river. "If we can't get the function room dried out and ready quickly, we'll lose all our Christmas party bookings, we just can't afford that and I'm not sure if the insurance will cover it yet. How soon can you get down here?"

Jenny grabbed her car keys, her camera and a notepad, "I'm on my way now." She hung up, locked the front door and jumped in the car.

As her car pulled up, she saw Derek watching out of the window for her. She rushed inside and he walked her through to the back of the hotel. The water was starting to drain away out of the function room, but there was a nasty tide mark on all of the walls and the carpet was ruined. They might be able to save some of the furniture, but the upholstered sofas and chairs had taken in a lot of water. She could see that Derek had slightly exaggerated when he said there was a foot of water, but even so the damage was considerable.

"The insurance assessors say they'll be here in the next few days," said Derek. "The water's starting to go down and as soon as we can get dried out, we'll need to get decorators in. Can you work up some designs and price it up so we're ready to go when that happens? Are you also able to project manage it? You've got all the contacts, haven't you?"

"Yes, yes and yes. Let me measure up and take some photos. Do you want to replace what you had before or update it? I assume you want something in keeping with the rest of the hotel," she asked.

"Um...err...similar to what we had before and bring it right up to date," Derek wasn't sure. "To be honest, I just want it in a fit state to be able to fulfill the party bookings."

Jenny's heart sank when she remembered the national magazines had shown an interest in photographing the hotel soon. In a way, this gave them the opportunity to really wow them. She only hoped they could be ready in time. She decided to wait before telling Derek this – he'd had enough bad news for now. Derek said that he'd leave her to do what she needed to do and he'd be in his office. Jenny dialed Debbie's number.

"Debbie, we've just had an order for a party of twelve and they're in a hurry!" Jenny said.

"That's quick." Debbie said understanding her 'code' immediately. Jenny explained what had happened. Now it was time to put Debbie's training as Head Chef to work.

Angela saw Nigel walking through the office clutching his laptop. "Here we go," she thought to herself. "This is the part where he shows Simon a 40 page slide presentation showing why he needs more staff."

"Hi Nigel," she smiled masking her thoughts. "Here for your meeting with Simon?"

"Yes. Is he ready?" Nigel asked.

Angela rose from her chair and walked to Simon's door. It was open and she stepped inside with Nigel behind her. "Nigel's here for his three o'clock with you."

Simon got up from his swivel chair and walked around his desk to meet him. Nigel was holding his laptop in his right hand and the charger in his left so Simon indicated the socket where he could plug in and recharge. Once connected, they settled into their seats at the meeting table.

"Thanks for seeing me," said Nigel. "I've been thinking about how to take the pressure off the support team and still be able to help users with their more advanced questions."

Simon prepared himself for a pitch about why they needed to increase their headcount. He was already thinking through his response, including a cookery related reference to keep the theme of his staff presentation going: *Too many cooks spoil the broth*, but he couldn't really make that one work here and it could be countered with *Many hands make light work*. Maybe he should steer clear of these kinds of sayings and clichés and actually focus on what Nigel was saying!

Nigel continued, "I've been going through the support requests for the last two months and the same things keep coming up. They aren't the sort of queries that are easily solved by an email exchange so they take longer than they should." Simon was thinking: any minute now, he'll ask for more staff. "We usually end up logging into the user's machine remotely to show them how to do whatever they need to do, but there's an easier way. Have a look at this."

He turned his laptop around to face Simon and clicked play. A video tutorial began to run showing which buttons to press to perform the task. It had a friendly female commentary. Within 90 seconds it was finished.

"To sort out a query like that generally takes 10-15 minutes if we do it the conventional way," Nigel pointed out. "This way it literally takes seconds and the user can watch it whenever they need it: 24 hours a day 7 days a week. If we started creating short videos like this now based on live support requests, we could have all the major queries addressed within three weeks, but I'd need to pull Laura – she's the voice you heard – off the support team temporarily."

Simon was astonished. This wasn't what he expected – he also hadn't realized they weren't already using video tutorials.

Nigel carried on, "This would mean that by the time the training courses are up and running, the basic level support requests could be dealt with automatically and we can devote more time to the advanced queries. It would also mean we can give users more time and deliver a higher level of customer service to them. Of course there will be some users who always want us to sort their problems out for them, but perhaps there is an opportunity there for more basic level training courses for new customers." Nigel stopped and looked at Simon.

Simon was lost for words. He knew he'd asked people to come to him with solutions, but this was really impressive. He realized he would have to change his stereotypical view of technical teams. "Nigel, I don't know what to say. This is very good indeed." He knew he would have to be sincere in his flattery. Nigel didn't seem the type to be impressed by over-enthusiasm. Simon stroked his chin thoughtfully as he repeated to himself, "yes, very good indeed. I like it. So Nigel, what do you need from me to get this moving?"

"Just the okay, really. We'd need to let Andy's team know that support is going to be a little bit slower initially, but as the videos come online we can start directing users to them. We'll need to hit a critical mass before putting them on the support site – it would be ridiculous to start sending people to it if there are only one or two videos," said Nigel.

"I think we also need to involve Rebekah and Karen," said Simon. "This will be a good message to get out to customers and prospects. Also Karen is preparing the content for the training courses, so she'll need to know what's available on the support site".

Simon and Nigel continued to talk and plan for how to communicate the new developments internally as well as to customers and users. As their discussions developed, they realized this was bigger than just the support team; there could be benefits all round – these videos could form the basis of in-house training too so everyone could be more familiar with the products the company sold.

When they were in the middle of deciding on time scales and deliverables Simon noticed Angela peeping in through the window in the door. His next meeting must be due to start. He glanced up at the clock on the wall. 4.07pm. The time had flown by. Rebekah must be ready to come in. This was a good opportunity to start the ball rolling, so he explained to Nigel and they invited her to join them. Nigel showed her the video and gave a quick summary of what had been discussed.

Rebekah too was impressed. This would give her another strong message to go with. Offering video tutorials wasn't exactly revolutionary, but the message that they could deliver a much higher level of support and spend time with users on their advanced queries, was something to shout about and differentiated them from competitors.

"Great, okay well I'll go and get the team started on this and we'll keep you updated with progress," said Nigel as he closed his laptop and reached down to unplug the charger. After he had left the room, Rebekah took the opportunity to let Simon know how the marketing activities were coming along.

"These are the brochures for the courses," she passed him print-outs of the documents that would be emailed out to customers. "I think the best approach is to telemarket them and then send the email once we have established interest. For those customers we either can't get hold of or are too busy to talk, we'll have an email marketing campaign around educating them about a few of the advanced features and showing the return in investment when they start using them. We can track who opens the emails and clicks on links so we can schedule a phone call out to them."

"That seems to make sense. Who's doing the telemarketing?" asked Simon.

"We'll do it in-house. The sales people already have a relationship with the customers and I got the impression from Andy they would be keen to do this," she said.

"Just so I'm clear, is Andy okay with this?" Simon asked.

"Yeah...I think so. This project was his idea after all," Rebekah sounded uncertain and Simon could see from her body language she was feeling uncomfortable and perhaps a little defensive.

"Shall we ask him before we go any further?" Simon got up from his seat, not expecting an answer to his rhetorical question. He dialed Andy's extension and asked if he could join them for a few minutes, which fortunately he could. Rebekah gulped. There was something about Andy which still intimidated her.

"Andy," said Simon, "come on in. Take a seat. Rebekah's been bringing me up to speed on the marketing plans. She's presented quite a comprehensive campaign and we'd like to get your help with some of it."

"Okay, can you talk me through it?" said Andy.

Rebekah shifted papers on the table and started to explain about the brochures, the email campaign, what was planned for social media and finally the telemarketing campaign. She missed out the part about Andy's team making the calls.

"All looks good to me apart from one thing," said Andy. "I think we should do the telemarketing in-house. I'm not comfortable with an outside company contacting our customers. We've already got the relationships with them and I don't want anyone else potentially undoing that. Plus the team can stress to customers that it will be good to meet them at the event," said Andy.

Rebekah opened her mouth to speak and Simon quickly responded in order to silence her, "I agree Andy, excellent idea. Are you sure they'll be able to manage the volume of calls?"

"Of course they will," huffed Andy. "They should be calling them regularly anyway. This is a good excuse to pick up the phone and find out how things are going. It's going to lead to more sales for them eventually so that's how I'll position it. Don't worry about the team; I'll get them on board. This isn't optional for them."

"Thanks Andy. Rebekah and I have a few more items to discuss and I'm sure Rebekah will see you tomorrow to work out the details, won't you?" Simon turned to Rebekah and she replied, "Yes."

When Andy was gone Simon apologized for talking over the top of her and explained, "Sometimes it's better for people to think something is their own idea. It gives them a sense of ownership and responsibility about it. They don't want to see their own idea fail." Simon was getting a strong sense of déjà vu and realized this was similar to a conversation he'd had with Sasha recently. One of the benefits of working with his coach was she was highly skilled in dealing with people - a talent Simon was starting to realize was crucial in a leadership position – and Sasha was a good teacher.

The following afternoon when Rebekah walked across the office to the sales team, she was surprised when a couple of people smiled at her and said hi. Just a few weeks ago, she'd wondered if she had somehow acquired the power of invisibility. "This is different," she thought and she liked how it made her feel, "people actually know my name!"

Andy greeted her with a smile at the door of his office.

"Sit down. I've briefed the team on making the calls about the courses and they're all fired up," Andy seemed proud of himself.

"That's fantastic. I wasn't sure how receptive they'd be. That's really good news," Rebekah figured a little flattery of his ego wouldn't go amiss and she was right.

Andy wanted to demonstrate how eager the team were as if to reinforce just what an achievement it had been to get them on board with doing the telemarketing. "They're actually keen to get going today if all the materials are ready."

"I can email the brochures over to you when we're done if you like," said Rebekah. "I've had a thought. Can you let me know as soon as you've got bookings? In my last company we used to include the logos of confirmed delegates on the brochures to show people who was already coming. It worked a treat, especially if you can get the big names confirmed first. People think: if it's good enough for them, it's good enough for us. Also, they don't like to think their competitors are getting one up on them by having more advanced knowledge," said Rebekah.

This made a lot of sense to Andy and he agreed to update her so she could add their logos to the brochures and the relevant pages of their website. He thought this approach of naming companies could work on the phone as well and made a mental note to tell the team.

He also realized he might have misjudged Rebekah. She seemed to have come out of her shell over the past weeks and was coming up with good suggestions. Maybe he should cut her some slack.

Their meeting over, Rebekah stopped to chat to Sanjay on her way back through the office. Andy couldn't quite make out what they were talking about. He assumed it was something to do with the materials the sales people would need at the training courses. He turned to his computer and looked up when he heard laughter. Andy saw Rachel, one of the other sales people, had joined the conversation. "She seems to be getting on well with the team," he thought and it dawned on him he had never heard Rebekah laugh before.

Recipe for Marketing a New Product

One of the toughest jobs for a marketer is to get people to try out a product or service for the first time, especially if it has just been launched.

While there is a small group of people known as 'early adopters' who will try something because it is new, the majority of buyers come in at the later stages once the merits of the product or service have been proven. Testimonials have long been used to show buyers what other people think of what you are offering. That is all well and good if you have a group of satisfied customers willing to let you publish their comments, but what if you are in the midst of launching a brand new product?

In the supermarket you may have been invited to try out a new drink or food item, at home you may have pulled out toiletry samples from magazines or received a new trial size item through your letterbox.

When you have a group of potential customers in one place – or even existing customers who you'd like to buy your new product – it's a little like offering a canapé or appetizer. Something which will whet their appetite without filling them up. After all, you would not want your sample to fully satisfy their needs or there is no reason for them to buy the full product!

In this recipe, you will see how making mini versions of traditional English Yorkshire puddings with roast beef and horseradish sauce can help you when developing your marketing plan.

Ingredients:
Eggs, pinch of salt, milk, plain flour, topside of beef, oil, horseradish sauce

Method:
To make the batter beat the eggs and salt together in a bowl, add half the milk and whisk in the flour until thick and free of lumps. Whisk in the rest of the milk, pour into a jug and leave to rest – Bring together all people tasked with communicating with the target audience and decide on the central message (USP or Unique Selling Proposition). The message needs to flow well and be lump free before taking the marketing message out into the marketplace. Allowing the message to 'rest' and for lumps to sink to the bottom gives everyone time to make sure the message is truly consistent and makes sense.

Preheat the oven and add a little oil to a roasting tin. Place the beef in the roasting tin and cook in the oven for 25-40 minutes. Remove the meat from the oven and allow to rest before carving – Cook just enough meat to give customers a taste of what you have in store for them. Take care to cook it to the preferences of your target market – some like beef cooked rare and others prefer it well-done. If they are impressed by the taster they are more likely to invest in the full product. You may not get a second chance to get it right.

Increase the heat in the oven. Pour a few drops of oil into each hole of a muffin or cup cake tin. Heat in the oven until the oil starts to smoke. Carefully pour the batter into each hole and bake until the puddings have puffed up and browned. Do not open the oven door or alter the heat until the puddings have browned or they will collapse – Some people say marketers are full of hot air and in this instance they may have a point! The marketing campaign needs to be intense enough to allow the message to rise in the customers' consciousness and to reach a point where it will stand up on its own, i.e. it reaches a tipping point where customers start talking about and recommending the product amongst themselves. Pull back on marketing too early or become complacent about the competition and the whole campaign is put in danger of deflating.

Carve the beef into thin slivers. Place a folded slice on the top of each mini-Yorkshire pudding. Add a little heap of horseradish sauce to the top of each one. Serve – Now that the message and the taster version of your product have been combined, it's time to start spreading the word. Reach out to people in your target market with a smile and offer them a taster. Be persistent, but also don't be offended if someone refuses – they might be vegetarian, on a diet or simply not hungry right now. If they have already eaten, it doesn't mean they won't be hungry again at some point in the future, so do stay in touch. Use your customer data to track those buyers who are still hungry (tried your taster, liked it and want more), are vegetarian (will never be in the market to buy what you offer), on a diet (budget-conscious but could be tempted with the right offering) or have already eaten (using another supplier). Keep in touch because 'no' usually means either 'not right now' or 'you haven't convinced me yet'.

FOOD FOR THOUGHT...

Small Changes Count

It is not always a big change to your business or business model that will produce the biggest impact on profitability. Often it is the impact of several small changes.

What follows is an example where if we can make small positive changes to various aspects of our business, they can have significant impact on your profitability. Unfortunately the reverse is also true. If the small changes are negative they can have a very detrimental effect on profitability.

While you may not be able to get a five percent improvement in all three areas (it may be more or less), whatever you can achieve will go straight to the bottom line.

FIND OUT MORE...
For more tips, tools and resources go to:
www.businesscookerybook.com/resources

		Before $	%	After $	%
1. Increasing sales by 5%	Sales	1,000,000	100	1,050,000	100
2. Reducing product cost by 5%	Cost of Sales	700,000	70	682,500	65
	Gross profit	300,000	30	367,500	35
3. Reducing overhead expenses by 5%	Overheads	200,000	20	190,000	18.1
Net profit will INCREASE by 77.5%	Net Profit	100,000	10	177,500	16.9

		Before $	%	After $	%
1. Decreasing sales by 5%	Sales	1,000,000	100	950,000	100
2. Product cost increased by 5%	Cost of Sales	700,000	70	712,500	75
	Gross profit	300,000	30	237,500	25
3. Overhead expenses increased by 5%	Overheads	200,000	20	210,000	22.1
Net profit will DECREASE by 72.50%	Net Profit	100,000	10	27,500	2.9

Chapter 10

Back at her desk at home, Jenny uploaded the photos of the function room to her computer so she could start working on ideas for Derek.

She took her phone out of her bag and put it on her desk. The display told her she'd had three missed calls. While she was at the hotel, she'd put the phone on silent and forgotten to turn the ringer back on. One missed call was her voicemail service and she didn't recognize the other two numbers but they were local.

She called voicemail first. The message was just the click of someone replacing the handset. "I really must change the greeting on my phone," she thought to herself. "I could be losing business if people don't know they've got through to me."

Before calling the other numbers back, she looked them up on a search engine. The first didn't appear, but the second one did – it was the main number for the Grand Valley Hotel.

She dialed the number and explained she had a missed call on her phone. Initially the reception staff were unsure who would have called her because all outgoing calls come from the same number. When she mentioned she was an interior designer, the penny dropped and they put her through to the General Manager's office.

The phone was answered, "Peter Forbes."

"Hello Mr. Forbes, my name is Jenny Richardson. I believe you called my number. I'm an interior designer."

"Ah yes, thank you for calling back and call me Peter. I saw the piece the paper ran on the refurbishment work you did. We've got a problem and I wanted to see if you can help," he said.

"If you can tell me more about the situation, I'll see what I can do," Jenny was curious now.

"With all the bad weather we've had a leak in the roof and unfortunately it's caused quite a lot of damage to two of our top floor bedrooms. Luckily we're far enough up the valley that we didn't get flooded, but our top floors are the larger suites and they are looking pretty shabby now. I'd been meaning to spruce them up anyway, so this gives us a perfect excuse. The frustrating thing is though that we may need to close the rest of the floor while the work is carried out because of the noise. I'm looking for someone who can work quickly. Does this sound like something you can help with?" he asked.

Jenny couldn't believe it – the piece in the paper had only run two days ago and already she potentially had two projects from it. "Yes Peter, this does sound like something I can help with. I can come down and see you tomorrow if that works for you."

"Okay, how about 10am?" he asked and they agreed to meet at that time.

Jenny was about to call Debbie to let her know, when it dawned on her that Peter hadn't asked how much she charged. It was almost always the first question people asked when they were interested in her designing their nursery or living room. "This is different," she thought.

She looked down at her notepad and saw the other number she'd missed a call from. She decided to ring them back first before calling Debbie.

"Hello?" said the woman's voice on the other end of the phone line. Jenny realized this was probably a residential number and her first impressions were that she sounded well-spoken.

"Good afternoon. My name is Jenny Richardson and it seems I may have missed a call from your number."

"Jenny Richardson...Jenny Richardson," she sounded thoughtful.

"I'm an interior designer," offered Jenny.

"You're the one from the newspaper. The one who worked on the hotel. Is that right?"

"Yes, that's right," replied Jenny.

"Do you also do residential work?" the woman asked.

"Yes, I do," answered Jenny.

"Oh good. We have just bought a little place on Church Lane and we'd like to have several of the rooms decorated. We are aiming for a modern, yet homely look in keeping with the house. Is that something you can help with?"

Jenny knew Church Lane and if it was the Church Lane she was thinking of, none of the country houses could be described as 'little places'. She told the woman she could probably help and would need to see the property first. She made an appointment to see her the day after tomorrow, made a note of her name, Mrs. Amanda Walker and her address.

Again Jenny reflected, "She didn't ask how much I charge".

Debbie sounded excited and apprehensive when Jenny explained about the three projects. This started to get Jenny worried. "Maybe I've bitten off more than I can chew," she wondered. When she was working at the department store as an interior designer, she didn't usually get too involved in project management and until now, all the projects she had worked on had been relatively small.

A few weeks later Jenny had won all three projects and continued to get enquiries resulting from the PR she had secured. She was fulfilling her role as Maître D' and getting the orders to the kitchen under the charge of Debbie the Head Chef and thought everything had been going well until she started to get complaints from clients. Dishes (elements of the project) were being served uncooked (unfinished), cold (late) or at the wrong time (in the wrong order).

Jenny spoke to her mum about it and between them they decided the best course of action would be to take on another assistant, but this time to find someone who already had experience in managing interior design projects. With hindsight, Jenny saw she had expected too much of Debbie. Debbie's skill was in administration, rather than managing contractors. While she had been keen to learn, it was Debbie who came to Jenny to say she didn't think she was cut out for this kind of work. The pressure on both of them was immense. Both hotels were keen to get the work done as quickly as possible because until it was finished, they were losing money. At least Mrs. Walker's project wasn't as urgent – or so she had thought. Seeing the project moving along, Mrs. Walker announced to them that she would be hosting a large party on Boxing Day and not only did the dining room need to be completed by then, the guest rooms also needed to be finished.

Jenny couldn't believe that she had taken on three projects at the same time with very similar deadlines.

She was in trouble.

~

The atmosphere was tense. A lot was riding on the success of this, the first of the company's open training courses. Rebekah summed it up when she turned to Simon and told him, "It feels like that last half hour before the party starts when everything's ready and you're still not sure if everyone's going to show up and have a good time."

He couldn't have put it better himself and thought everything had turned out just as Jenny's mum had described. This event was the dinner party that everything had been leading up to. The invitations had gone out and guests had confirmed. The dishes were prepared, the table was set and now it was time for the guests to arrive. "Let's hope we don't end up giving anyone food poisoning!" Simon thought to himself.

He glanced out into the corridor and saw three people making their way towards the training room. Ducking back inside, he indicated to Paula who was handling registrations that people had started to arrive. She shuffled the name badges on the table in front of her and looked down the delegates list. For a first course, the list was impressive. Their key customers had sent at least one of their staff and some had sent more. The various teams had done well and really pulled together to make this work. As Simon reminded himself, it wasn't time to congratulate themselves just yet. That would come at the end of the day when the feedback forms were in.

In the half hour before the course was due to start there was a steady trickle of delegates arriving and with ten minutes to go, he realized that only half of the people who were supposed to be there had arrived. He didn't want to start late, but struck up a conversation with one of the delegates who mentioned that she had been wandering around the building for about fifteen minutes before finding the correct room. He asked her to excuse him and decided to investigate for himself. He walked out towards the reception area planning to walk the route again, pretending he didn't know where he was going. Straight away he could see something was amiss. He couldn't see the event listed on the board and asked a member of staff. They couldn't find the event he was talking about! He tried the company name, nothing. He tried the title of the course, nothing. Eventually he asked by the name of the room the course was happening in.

"Ah yes sir, I have it" said Sebastian on the front desk. "You are the Advanced Software Training event, yes?"

"Yes, but that's not what people will be looking for," Simon said angrily. He corrected the name on the sheet and demanded the event board be updated immediately and for signs to be put up showing delegates the way.

Simon stomped back towards the training room. Paula was still signing people in so he headed for Ian, one of the salespeople who were on-site to help customers. It was quite obvious that Ian wasn't interested in customers at all today. He was chatting away to Caroline, another salesperson, and - judging from their smiles and body language - appeared to be flirting with her. They had moved over to the corner of the room and seemed oblivious to everything going on around them. Simon could almost feel his blood boiling.

"You two, come with me," he grunted and walked out into the corridor with the expectation they would follow him. They shrugged at each other and joined him in the corridor. "We've got delegates wandering the building looking for this room and we're due to start in five minutes. Please can one of you go to reception to meet and greet and send them in this direction, and the other one of you start rounding people up." It wasn't a question; he expected them to do it. They both looked flustered and Caroline blushed. "I'd like you to do it now please," he added and they trotted off towards reception.

Andy had seen the exchange from across the room and broke off from his conversation to find out what was going on, "Problem?"

"Yes there's a problem," said Simon. "The venue has messed up the booking name, we've got people wandering lost in the building looking for 'Advanced Software Training' and those two were too busy chatting each other up to notice. I've sent them to round people up and bring them through."

"Okay, if you'd let me know, I'd have dealt with it. Let's focus on the 31 people we do have here in the room and make sure they feel welcome. Sanjay over there is doing a great job, he's a natural networker – the rest of the team could learn a lot from him. When he made that suggestion about how to look after the customers and up-sell, he knew what he was talking about. I haven't seen him in action since I trained him 18 months ago and he's turned into a real star. Anyway," Andy continued, "isn't it time for your welcome address?"

"I suppose so. I'm not sure I'm in the right mood for it now, do you want to lead and I'll say something?" Andy was surprised, but because they were running out of time, he went ahead with the welcome.

Four days later and the family were in the car heading to Granny and Grandpa's house for Sunday lunch. It had been an effort to get the children ready and once on their way, Simon began to understand why.

"Granny hates me," sulked Noah.

"She doesn't hate you darling. What on earth makes you think that?" asked Jenny.

"She's always tells me off and shouts at me," he sounded upset.

Jenny and Simon looked at each other puzzled. Simon was driving, so Jenny turned to face Noah in the back seat. "When does she shout at you darling?"

"All the time." This wasn't helping.

"What does she say?"

Noah shrugged his shoulders and looked out of the window. Jenny turned back around and shrugged to Simon. He could feel the thud, thud, thud of Rosie's feet in his back as she swung them and was grateful his parents didn't live too far away. He pulled up the car outside the house and said, "Okay kids we're here," as he turned off the engine. Noah groaned.

They walked up the path to the house together and Simon's father Malcolm opened the front door to them.

"Hi Dad," Simon said as he reached out to shake his hand.

"Come on son," Malcolm said as he pulled him closer for a manly hug. He winked over Simon's shoulder to Jenny and the kids.

"Where's Mum?" Simon asked.

Malcolm rolled his eyes, "In the kitchen, where she's been since about seven this morning. I offered to help, but you know her. Nothing I do is right. I've left her to it and been sorting out the shed." He bent forward and looked at Noah and Rosie in turn. "Now then, who are these grown up children? What have you done with Noah and Rosie?"

"It's us Grandpa!" Rosie shrieked and grabbed his leg. Malcolm playfully tried to shake her off and walked back into the house with her standing on his foot as he swung her with every step. Noah said nothing and peeped past him.

"What are you looking for Noah?" Malcolm asked.

"Nothing."

"He thinks Granny doesn't like him," Jenny whispered to Malcolm.

Malcolm whispered back to her, "We all feel like that sometimes" and winked at Noah, who smiled.

Rita emerged from the kitchen drying her hands on a tea towel. "Hello darling," she kissed her son on the cheek, "and hello Jenny. Noah! Rosemary!" She knelt down to the children's level.

"My name's Rosie," a small voice said.

"Rosie is short for Rosemary," Rita explained as she patted her on the head and stroked her hair. "Rosemary's your proper name."

Noah did his best to stay out of reach, but she spotted him. "Noah, come here and give Granny a kiss." He shook his head. "Don't be silly, come and give me a kiss." He shook his head again.

Jenny whispered, "He's a bit shy today." Noah glared at his mum.

"Something smells good," said Simon as he walked through the house to the kitchen. Noah went with him. The door to the kitchen swung back and forth. Through it Rita could see Simon looking out towards the tree in the garden and...

"Noah, NO!" Rita rushed through to the kitchen just in time to stop him pulling a saucepan of boiling water onto him – or so she thought. Simon turned sharply with a look of horror on his face. Noah's eyes began to well up and he ran out of the kitchen into his mother's arms.

It took a while for Jenny to soothe Noah and she started to see how he might think Granny didn't like him. In actual fact she cared deeply about him and had been trying to protect him from injuring himself, she just didn't know how to show him. In all the time she had known Rita, the only time she had even seen her show any form of maternal affection was to Simon.

She'd asked Simon years ago about this. He reluctantly explained that his younger cousin David - Rita's sister Ros's boy - had badly broken his leg in childhood after falling from a tree in their garden. David had been in and out of hospital for two years as they tried to fix the damage; Ros had never forgiven Rita for taking her eyes off the boys while they played in her garden. Since then, she had been over-protective.

Noah looked very much like his father and Jenny now wondered if Noah reminded Rita of David. Noah's reluctance to kiss Granny probably hurt her deeply.

She also wondered why Rita insisted on calling Rosie Rosemary. Did the name Rosie remind her of Ros? Maybe.

There was no more time for thinking now. Simon walked through to the lounge where Jenny had been cuddling Noah and calming him down. "Food's nearly ready. Are you coming through?" Simon said. Jenny nodded and kissed Noah in his forehead.

"Yes, we're coming, aren't we Noah?" and followed Simon into the dining room.

Most of the food was already in bowls on the table. Malcolm was standing proudly over the roast beef brandishing the carving knife.

Rita was in the kitchen preparing the rest of the food. She poked her head past the swing door and said, "Don't wait for me. Start serving up." This always made Simon uncomfortable. His mum had always instilled in him that you should wait until everyone was seated before starting your meal, so he continued to wait. Jenny didn't and started passing plates around with roast potatoes, vegetables, and the meat Malcolm had just carved.

Rita came out of the kitchen with the rest of the food, which was piping hot. Noah copied his mother and reached for the bowl Rita had just put on the table. "Don't touch that," Rita barked. "It's hot."

Jenny could see Noah's eyes redden and his lip start to tremble. "Darling," she said to Noah softly. "Do you see Granny's wearing oven gloves?" He nodded. "That's because the bowl's hot and if you touched it with bare hands it'd burn you. Granny just wants to keep you safe. She loves you very much. Isn't that right Granny?"

Now it was Rita's turn to well up. "Yes, that's right D...Noah. Granny loves you very much," and she walked round the table to give him a cuddle. This time he didn't run away. "Noah," she looked him in the eye, "it frightens me when I see you doing things that might hurt you. I don't want to see you in pain and I want to keep you safe. I'm sorry I shouted at you." Noah gave a half-smile and cuddled her. Rita found it hard to let him go, but she pulled herself away. "Gravy," she said. "I need to get the gravy" and she walked out into the kitchen.

After a few minutes, she still hadn't returned and plates were starting to empty. Jenny got up and went through to the kitchen where she found Rita sniffing, wiping her eyes and staring at the tree in the garden. The gravy was still unmade. For the first time, she put her arm around her and Rita started to cry. She sat her down at the kitchen table.

"I'm sorry Jenny. I've ruined what should have been a lovely meal together," sobbed Rita.

"It's alright, mum." Rita looked up. "Mum?"

"Well, you're my second mum," Jenny smiled.

"I like that."

"I know you care a lot about Noah and Rosie. It feels like you hold back sometimes though." She wasn't quite sure how to phrase what she was about to say. "Do they remind you of what happened with David?"

Jenny could see she had struck a nerve and was right, yet Rita denied it. "David?" she pretended not to know what Jenny was talking about. "Oh, do you mean my nephew David? I assume Simon told you about his fall from the tree. No, it's nothing to do with that. I just don't want either of the children to get hurt while they're here."

Malcolm swung open the door and interrupted their conversation. He looked at the unmade gravy, "shall I finish the gravy off? There are hungry people in the dining room!"

Rita got up, "No, you leave it, I'll do it. You two go back in and eat; I'll be there in a minute." Jenny and Malcolm did as they were told and Rita soon came through with the gravy, and then turned back to the kitchen.

"Mum, aren't you eating?" Simon asked.

"No, I need to get the dessert ready. I'm not all that hungry anyway," she said while swinging the door and disappearing into the kitchen. Malcolm rolled his eyes out of sight of her, but in plain sight of everyone at the table.

"So, Simon, how's your new job going?" Malcolm asked.

Later that evening after the children were in bed, Jenny and Simon had time to talk about the day's events.

"You know, it's a pity Mum kept disappearing into the kitchen. I wanted to tell her about how everything's going at work. She encouraged me to take the job and in the last few months hasn't asked about it at all," said Simon.

"I think she had a few things on her mind today," Jenny said.

"Even so, she invited us over. All she seemed to do was hang around behind the scenes, occasionally coming out to bark and upset people and then complain later that she'd hardly seen us and had been on her feet all day. She never lets Dad help and that's why she ends up so tired. The thing is, I don't really care about the food all that much, I wanted to spend time with my parents, but she seems to think the food is the most important thing and hides away in the kitchen. She's my mum and I wanted to talk to her."

Suddenly he realized the parallels with how he'd behaved at the training course. There might have been customers there who wanted to talk to him, but in his haste to sort out the problem with the signs at the venue, he'd completely ignored them. It could have been a valuable opportunity to find out firsthand about how the customers were using their software, to build relationships and generate good 'PR' - and he'd wasted it.

Jenny could see he was in mid-thought, but had to ask, "What's up? What are you thinking?"

Simon paused before replying, "God help me. I'm turning into my mum!"

Recipe for Customer Service

Customers' experiences of our service depend on many things all of which need to be well thought out by our organizations. Like the recipe below for stir fry there is a great deal of time needed for preparation but the cooking time is quick, similar to how our customers make up their mind about us.

The stir fry dish needs to be colorful, make the right impression and keep the vegetables crunchy. Our preparation might be spot on but the dish can still be ruined in the few seconds we are doing the cooking. Likewise our customer service can fail at the point of delivery.

Ingredients:
Flank steak, red bell peppers, straw mushrooms, broccoli, Marinade: sherry, soy sauce, minced ginger, green onion Other: garlic, beef or chicken broth, cornstarch mixed in water, sugar, oil for stir frying.

Method:
Partly freeze the meat, Cut across grain into slices – Taking these actions helps ensure the meat is easy to cut and we get the strips nice and even. Working out how to deliver great customer service in a cost effective way can depend on our approach particularly at the beginning.

Cut the bell pepper in half and remove the stem and any seeds. Then cut into thin strips – We need to understand what is important to the customer and strip away those things that the customer puts no value on.

Rinse the mushrooms under warm running water and slice – We may need to soften up our customers by ensuring that our service is ongoing and not one off.

Cut broccoli into bite size pieces – Not everybody likes broccoli so we must make sure that it does not overpower the impression the dish makes on the eater, Hence we cut it into bite sized pieces. It may even require us to switch the broccoli with another vegetable like green beans.

Combine the meat with the sherry, soy sauce, ginger and green onion. Marinade for 30 minutes – The marinade is going to have a significant influence on how the meat tastes and its impact on the overall taste of the dish. Likewise the environment in which the client interacts with us will be an important part of his/her experience.

Heat a wok and add oil. When the wok is hot add garlic and stir fry until fragrant. Add the sliced beef, brown briefly and then stir fry until it is cooked through. Push up the side of the wok – All the parts are starting to come together here. We need to make sure everyone in our organization understands that they are part of the customer's over all experience. Whether it is the person who answers the phone, the salesperson or the provider they all have a part to play.

Add oil to wok, add broccoli and stir fry briefly. Then add the mushrooms and red peppers – This is where the color comes in. What can we add to our customer service that will improve the impression we give.

Add beef broth and the cornstarch/water. Turn up heat and stir to thicken. Sprinkle the sugar on top – This is going to put the gloss on our ingredients and will definitely have an impact on the impression the dish makes. You need to ask yourself what would put the gloss on your customer service and will it help the overall impression the customer gets.

Mix everything together and serve hot with rice or noodles – It's all coming together now and the proof will be in the eating. Like in our business if everybody has played their part we will have excellent customer service.

FOOD FOR THOUGHT...

Understanding customer types

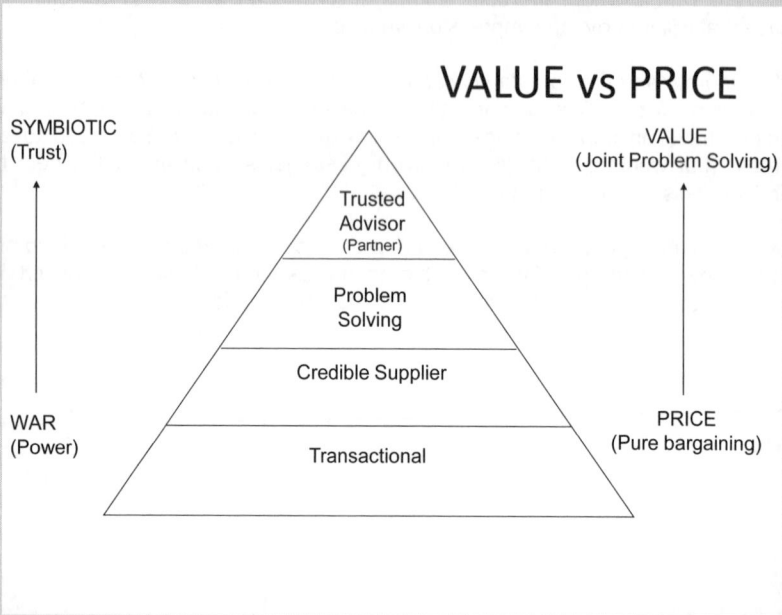

VALUE vs PRICE

SYMBIOTIC
(Trust)

VALUE
(Joint Problem Solving)

Trusted
Advisor
(Partner)

Problem
Solving

Credible Supplier

WAR
(Power)

Transactional

PRICE
(Pure bargaining)

It is vital that we can categorize our customers by types because this will give us a better understanding of their contribution to our profitability. In many cases the Pareto principle applies to the profit contributions of various types of customers. This basically says that 20% of our customers contribute 80% of our profits and conversely that 80% of our customers contribute 20% of our profits.

The more trust there is in the relationship and the more value the customer sees us contributing to his business, the higher the likely profit will be on business transacted with them. On this basis we want to try and move our customers up the triangle.

In the beginning the relationship is more transactional with the buyer having the power in the relationship. As we add value and build trust we can move a transactional customer to see us as a credible supplier, then maybe a problem solver for them and finally to being a trusted advisor. The relationship becomes more symbiotic.

It is therefore most important to know each customers profit contribution to your business. This does not just mean the margin on the transaction but also needs to take into account the cost of serving them from a selling point of view, cost of credit and any other costs directly related to that customer.

You may find that a customer that you think is profitable for you may after taking all costs into account may be actually costing you money.

FIND OUT MORE...

For more tips, tools and resources go to:
www.businesscookerybook.com/resources

Chapter 11

Jenny seemed to be speaking to her mum most weeks getting help with the business. She felt lucky to have such a wonderful mentor and didn't know what she would have done without her. She had met several small business coaches and mentors at networking events in the past and some had really impressed her. At the time, she hadn't appreciated just how useful if could be to have someone outside of the business looking in objectively and providing timely support and guidance.

As she thought about it, one of the most valuable things her mum did was to help her make decisions about what to do next. On her own, Jenny wasn't the greatest decision-maker. She could always see both sides of an argument and kept searching for new options all the time. Working with her mum had taught her that you often need to just make a decision and get on with things.

That's how it had happened with the PR. Left to her own devices, Jenny could have procrastinated over it or worse listened to what her mum told her and then decided to tweak it, rendering Barbara's proven recipe ineffective. The thing with recipes is that you can only start tinkering with them when you've worked through them a few times and know what you're doing. Jenny had learned there was real value in taking a recipe and following the instructions to the letter. She had done exactly as she was told and now had more business than she could handle on her own!

The projects were progressing well. She had placed an advertisement for an assistant and been inundated with applications from people trying to break into interior design. Jenny was adamant she needed someone with prior experience, so she was able to filter the applications on that basis. Eventually she hired Wendy, who had previously worked for a small firm of architects, and she was able to hit the ground running. It had made such a difference to both Jenny and Debbie – they could each concentrate on the work they were good at and were supposed to be doing.

Wendy got straight onto the contractors and made sure Derek's hotel was able to open on time and he was able to hold the Christmas parties. That was not her only motivation. An important national glossy magazine confirmed they wanted to feature the hotel and it needed to be ready for the shoot so they could make the April edition.

Jenny started to track when each piece of publicity was due to come out so they could be ready for the flurry of enquiries that followed. She had also started scanning the features and including them on her website so that it not only had her portfolio on there, but the logos of the publications she had appeared in and copies of the articles.

Over the past few months Jenny felt like her business had really grown up.

Derek had been delighted with the work her company had done for him and also for the publicity she had generated. He had ordered stand-up cards showing the editorial features for the reception area and for every room. Far from it coming across as bragging, the customers seemed to really like the fact they were staying in a 'famous' hotel.

"Mum," Jenny said during one of their catch-ups on the phone, "do you remember months ago you telling me how to run a dinner party?"

"Yes, I do," said Barbara.

"I don't know if you realized it at the time, but you were also giving me the recipe for improving my business! Simon's been using it in his business too and it seems to be working very well."

A month after the training course, the senior team assembled to assess how it had gone. All agreed it had been worthwhile and they waited to hear about the numbers.

Simon started off. "I've been going through the feedback forms from the delegates and the general opinion is that they got a lot out of the course. There were some points where we can improve next time, such as the organization with the venue, but on the whole it was very positive."

Everyone was in agreement. Now to hear about the numbers and Simon nodded to Diane that it was time to hear from her.

She passed around a spreadsheet and did a running commentary on the figures. "When you look at the money spent on the organization and promotion of the course and compare that to the revenue, we made a slight profit." The team smiled. She pointed out, "What hasn't been factored in is the labor involved and the opportunity cost, in other words, what didn't get done because the course took place. There was a definite impact on product sales with the team being focused on inviting delegates rather than developing leads." Andy started to speak, but Simon raised his hand to stop him so Diane could continue. "Of course, what we can't put a value on is the goodwill and future business which will come as a result of the course. It's too early to tell."

Andy couldn't wait any longer and said, "It's not too early to tell. Sanjay picked up a referral from one of his customers and is having a sales meeting with them as we speak. He has also followed up with several of the delegates who have asked for proposals for running the course in-house for them. This is something which we'd struggled to sell previously. Based on his closing rate, I'd say we will finish next month at least 15% up on this month. The rest of the sales team have had similar experiences, so I'd say it was definitely worthwhile. If we put most of our marketing budget into running these events rather than advertising in magazines, we'd do a lot better. Sorry Rebekah, nothing personal, just an observation this gives a better return on investment."

Rebekah spoke up, "I was actually about to say something very similar. Diane mentioned it's difficult to put a value on goodwill. It's also difficult to put a value on our brand. If we could, I'd expect that its value increased significantly after the course. It's shifted how our customers see us. It helped us stand out from our competitors and gave us all the opportunity to talk to them face to face. In our line of business, referrals and recommendations are incredibly valuable and anything that generates as many referrals as this did should be repeated."

She wondered whether she should make her next comment and decided she should. "I'll put my hands up and admit I made the wrong call to focus so heavily on advertising." Andy raised an eyebrow. She added, "There is a place for those magazines in our plan, but I'm sure we can get equal if not better coverage if we approach it editorially and do follow-up success stories with our customers who went on the course, used the advanced features and have seen it have a positive impact on their organization."

There was silence around the table.

Simon decided it was down to him to speak next. "Thank you Rebekah, it's good to know you and Andy are in agreement on this. The plan to switch from advertising to PR sounds sensible. We can work out all the details separately."

Simon turned to Nigel who was not usually included in these meetings, but he felt needed to be kept informed about what was happening. As Technical Support Manager his team would be dealing with the queries resulting from the course. "Nigel, could you give us an update please on the video tutorials?"

"We've recorded and uploaded 23 videos now covering the most frequently asked questions and problems. They've been in place for five days and being able to send people to a video is currently saving each member of the team about half an hour a day. Once users get accustomed to finding the answers for themselves I think it's likely to save two to three hours a day per member of staff. This means we're going to be free to provide more advanced support. It's interesting to hear what Andy said about being asked for more in-house training courses. There are a couple of people on my team who are excellent trainers and with the time we save through having the videos, we could run the in-house training for customers. It would save us a lot of money when you compare it to bringing in outside trainers who don't know the software as well."

Karen couldn't help but feel like her nose had been put a little out of joint. While Nigel didn't mean it, the implication was that she had been wasting money by bringing in external trainers when there was resource within the company. She knew she was overreacting. Until five days ago there was no way the company could have released members of the technical support team to run courses. Nigel's solution was actually brilliant. She decided to keep quiet other than to say, "Good idea."

Rebekah added to the discussions, "The other thing we can do better next time is to include the comments from the feedback forms on the marketing materials and the logos from the customers. It will help people to get sign off from their managers to go on the course if they can show them who else has done it."

"This is all sounding good," said Simon. "So, are we decided that we'll do this again?"

The answer was a unanimous yes.

Recipe for Effective Follow-Up & Analysis

Each time an organization invests time and resources into a new activity, lessons can be learned. Of course this is provided the people involved take the time to learn those lessons - what worked and what could be done better, whether to run the activity again or whether to put it down to experience, and last but by no means least whether the activity was profitable.

Unfortunately in many organizations a great number of activities run concurrently leaving little time for analysis.

They say '*you are what you eat*'.

This applies to organizations as well. The mood, culture and the extent to which people are engaged can be dictated by what and *how* you eat. Rushing a meal usually results in indigestion. Racing from one activity to another without pause for thought usually means that key learning points are overlooked and people end up uncomfortable and bloated.

Various medical studies over the years have shown a Mediterranean diet to have health benefits. We like to think that the Mediterranean *way* of eating contributes to those health benefits.

Traditional Mediterranean mealtimes offer a more relaxed way of eating. Families and friends come together to share their news and their problems and people take time to savor each mouthful.

In Spain, the custom is to eat dinner from around 9-11pm, so *tapas* bars serve food which can be enjoyed in a relaxed environment with friends on the way back home. Tapas dishes are varied and light enough that they can be eaten without spoiling an appetite. The emphasis is on discussion and sharing, very much like the follow-up and analysis after a key business event.

Enjoying Spanish Tapas at home
The idea with tapas is to give people something to talk about and compare notes. Each person will have different tastes, so give them the opportunity to try new things out and discuss what they like and dislike with their colleagues. Serve a selection of dishes and encourage people to try all of them.

Cold Food

Ingredients:
Selection of sliced cured meats such as chorizo, black olives and crusty bread.

Method:
Serve on separate dishes – people tend to consume more if dishes are served separately rather than all on one plate. This is because helping yourself to a lot of food from one plate can come across as being greedy. You can encourage people to engage more in discussions if you break topics down into bite sized portions.

Hot Food

Calamari:
Ingredients:
Squid cut into rings, oil, flour, salt, mayonnaise, lemon.

Method:
Pour enough olive oil into a wok or large open frying pan so that the oil will be deep enough to cover the calamari rings, and put on high heat. While the oil is heating, place a couple handfuls of flour and a pinch of salt into a large plastic bag or sandwich bag. Place a few rings into the bag, seal the bag and shake to cover the rings with flour. Remove the rings one at a time and carefully place in the hot oil – continue with all pieces. Fry until the rings turn golden. When done, remove carefully from pan and drain briefly on a paper towel. Serve while hot with lemon and mayonnaise - Calamari is a simple dish to prepare, but cooking with hot oil can be dangerous if you have too many people in the kitchen. In the same way some inflammatory business topics are better dealt with away from any environments where you want people to relax and share constructive information with one another. When calamari is served, it is often confused with onion rings by people unfamiliar with Mediterranean cooking. Likewise when conducting the follow-up after a business activity, be very clear about which aspect you are talking about to avoid any confusion.

FOOD FOR THOUGHT...

Focusing on profit, not cash flow

It is very easy to become overly focused on profit; after all, it's the profit that makes your business successful, right? To a certain extent the answer to this question is "yes", but to an equal extent the answer to this question is certainly "no". Profit is important, but cash flow is just as important if not more important. A great number of very profitable companies end up failing and going under because they pay too much attention to profit and not enough attention to cash flow. They simply run out of money.

Fortunately there are some very easy and straightforward things you can do to improve cash flow and keep it flowing consistently. Examples include:

Be cautious about offering deferred payments to your customers. While this might be a good way to entice them into buying a high priced/high profit margin item, it also reduces the actual cash flowing into your business. In many cases it is better (and less complicated) to set the price lower and accept a lower profit margin because it allows you to get the money from the customer up front.

For those items that are high value, make a point of taking a deposit from the customer when they make the purchasing decision. This makes it less likely that the customer will change their mind, but just as importantly, it helps to cover any costs you incur up front. For instance, you might have to buy extra stock, pay staff to work on the project, or otherwise spend money at the beginning of the transaction that you won't be able to recover until the end point.

If the process takes an extended length of time you could easily find yourself very low on the cash you need to keep the business operating.

Whenever possible, ask for payment in advance. This is especially important when working with a new customer who has yet to establish a good record of timely payment. At the very least, get as much as possible in advance and set benchmarks at various points in the process; every time a benchmark is reached, the customer makes another payment.

In these days of very difficult economic conditions, more and more individuals and companies are delaying payments on their debts as long as possible. While it's certainly understandable that they may be struggling, you must not let their cash flow problems become your cash flow problems. Set up a procedure to identify late payers as early as possible, and take whatever action is necessary to recover those debts sooner rather than later.

You might be tempted to ease your cash flow situation by taking on higher levels of debt. This is a risky, expensive, and potentially very damaging approach so you should do whatever you can to avoid it. Plan ahead during peak times when cash flow is good by setting aside extra money; this will give you a reservoir of cash to tap into during the inevitable slow times, allowing you to steer clear of taking on too much debt.

Finally, give serious thought to leasing or renting your operating premises and equipment rather than buying them. This gives you much greater flexibility with your cash because instead of tying it up in assets which cannot be easily liquidated, you can keep it in a form that is more quickly and easily accessible when it is needed.

FIND OUT MORE...

For more tips, tools and resources go to:
www.businesscookerybook.com/resources

Chapter 12

"Jenny, very good to see you," said Peter Forbes, General Manager of the Grand Valley Hotel. He saw the camera in her hand. "I see you've come well-prepared."

"Hello Peter, yes I think so," said Jenny and they walked towards the lift together.

"Thank you so much for getting everything finished so quickly. You've got a good team," said Peter as they arrived at the top floor of the hotel. The doors opened, "after you."

In the middle of winter, there wasn't much natural light in the bedrooms, so they switched all the lamps on so Jenny could get the photos she needed.

"These ones are just for the website. The magazines will want to send their own photographers with professional lighting equipment," Jenny explained. She was going to use the same recipe again to get publicity from this project. When she had told Peter how much interest the piece for Derek's hotel generated, he was very keen to get this for his hotel as well. They were different kinds of hotels with different clientele, so were not in direct competition.

"Jenny, while you're here, there's something I've been meaning to talk to you about," said Peter.

Jenny didn't like the sound of this. It sounded like the opening line to a complaint, so she braced herself and replied, "Oh, what's that?"

"The company that owns this hotel is in the process of acquiring a small group of four hotels in the surrounding counties. They've been under-performing for years and once the deal goes through – which is due to be in the next 10 days - they'll need to be brought up to standard. The décor's a bit dated now," Peter paused to gauge Jenny's reaction and to make sure he had her full attention. He continued,

"It's going to be a big job and we'll need to have someone we trust on board. I'll be straight with you. The work you did on the bedrooms was effectively your interview. If you did well with that, you were going to be in the running for the larger project. I'm sorry I couldn't be more open with you from the start, but I needed to know how you really worked, not how you'd work if you knew you might get a bigger project from it."

"That's okay, I completely understand," said Jenny, not knowing if she was going to be offered the work or told she'd failed the interview.

"If you're interested, we'd like to offer you the contract to completely refurbish all four hotels over the next three years."

"Are you serious?" Jenny couldn't believe her ears.

"Yes," Peter smiled, "I'm deadly serious."

"I don't know what to say!"

"Yes would be a good start," said Peter.

"Yes!" they both laughed.

"We can work out the details once the deal has gone through, so I'd be grateful if you would keep this confidential until then," said Peter.

"Of course," said Jenny. All of a suddenly a wave of panic hit her when she thought about the amount of work she would need to do and her commitment to covering Nicole's maternity leave, which was due to start soon. "Peter," she said, "it sounds like this is going to be an extensive project. I work closely with a firm of architects and they could certainly help here."

"That's TVR Associates, isn't it?" Peter was sure she had told him this already, or did he find the information out when he did his background research on her? He couldn't remember clearly. Jenny nodded and looked puzzled as if she wasn't sure how he knew. He continued, "We can talk about that when we work out the details. I'd appreciate it if you didn't talk to them about it yet. Is that okay?"

"Yes, that's okay," said Jenny.

For the rest of the day she thought she was going to burst with excitement, unable to tell anyone what was going on. Her head was buzzing with questions and ideas. This would take her business to a whole new level!

Two months on from the course and plenty had changed. Andy's team had set themselves a target to personally speak to each of the delegates to follow up with them and see how they were getting on. Largely, they had succeeded.

What had interested the team was just how quickly people seemed to forget what they had learned if they didn't use it straight away. They noticed that the retention of what they had been taught was greatest when several users from the same company had been trained together. It allowed them the chance to ask each other how to do things and they could influence how the company used the software.

The best results came from the companies where they invested in in-house training. That didn't surprise anyone.

It would have been tempting to say that the company should only focus on getting in-house training work, but without the open courses being available as 'tasters' the sales team would struggle to sell them as they had before.

No, the best approach seemed to be to run the open courses, with a view to up-selling when people had tried out and seen the benefits. Somewhat like the samples of new brands available at the supermarket. Getting people to try a new brand or product can be tough, unless you heavily discount (but discounting tends to attract the most fickle and disloyal customers) or allow them to sample it first.

Simon reflected on the past months as he prepared his presentation for the Board of Directors. It was time for his review meeting and he knew this was the time when his performance as a Managing Director was under scrutiny. He felt satisfied that what he done with the company since his appointment reflected well not only on him, but on his staff.

Sales were up, profitability was up and staff retention had improved dramatically. Before he joined their better people had been easily tempted by offers at other companies, but he'd heard from

Karen this was no longer the case. When head hunters called senior people offering them interviews for other positions, his staff had usually gone along out of curiosity and then decided to stay with the company. Karen's network of contacts within the industry was strong enough that she often heard of these approaches through the grapevine. The staff involved probably never knew that she knew and she certainly wasn't going to tell them.

Simon prepared dull chart after dull chart and found he was losing enthusiasm for his presentation. He decided he needed some fresh air and a new perspective, so picked up his laptop, wrapped up warm and set off to the coffee shop over the road to work from there.

He settled at a table close to the coffee machine. It was noisy, but it was in the warmest area of the shop. From where he sat he found himself watching the baristas and the processes going on in the coffee shop. He saw how they took orders, prepared drinks, heated up food and served the customers. This gave him the inspiration he was looking for.

He searched on his laptop for the presentations the directors had delivered to staff a couple of months ago – the ones with the cookery themes. He also cast his mind back to that fateful conversation with Jenny even longer ago about using the dinner party analogy in business.

He could use the example of a dinner party to show what he had done and get the Board's support in implementing the next phase of the business.

He pulled out a notepad and started to map out on paper the different areas he and his staff had worked on together.

These are the headings he came up with when he thought about the training courses:

Vision & Mission – be clear about the purpose of your dinner party, what are you trying to achieve? They had set out to build relationships with customers to the point where they could up-sell more easily.

Know your market – who do you want at your dinner party? They wanted to speak directly to the users and decision-makers within the companies who used their software

Find out what they want – what do people like to eat? Do they have any allergies or preferences? He, Andy, Rebekah and the sales team had invested time in asking their customers what they actually wanted.

Make a plan – which dishes are you going to serve? Which recipes are you going to follow? Initially, some of the team thought this could be done at the last minute, but with Rebekah's insistence they had all come to realize they needed to make decisions on the content of the courses – the dishes they would serve - much earlier in the process.

Practice and learn from others – don't expect to cook a new dish brilliantly the first time. Get used to the ingredients, how the oven works and the timings involved. Get help from people who already know how to cook the dish. The team had enlisted the help of experts who could guide them in the right direction and stop them making mistakes. They had also utilized the experience within the company and given a voice to those who had previously been ignored and overlooked.

Get the right suppliers – Which ingredients and utensils do you need? How do they work? They had brought together all the elements of running the course and introduced new systems.

Share the workload – work out who can chop, peel, stir, serve the dish and wait on the guests. If necessary, get caterers in to help or buy pre-prepared food. They had got practically every department involved and bought in the expertise of others outside the company.
Lead and communicate – make sure everyone knows which parts they play in the dinner party. Once the senior team was agreed on how everything would work, they held the staff meeting to present the strategy and also made it clear that they were open to suggestions

on how to take it forward. This had been the catalyst for automating much of the technical support function and helping staff to contribute their ideas.

Spread the word – send out the invitations to guests so they keep the date free and get them excited about coming to the dinner party. The marketing had been highly personalized so each 'guest' had felt valued. They had also told each 'guest' who else was definitely coming.

Customer service is key – you can't leave your guests alone to look after themselves. You need to be present at the dinner table and engage with them. While he had fallen down on this area personally, most members of the sales team had taken the initiative and cared for the delegates well while they were at the course. The technical support team had thought ahead and prepared for providing a higher level of support for users after the course.

Follow-up and referrals – contact each guest thanking them for coming and many will tell their friends what a good time they had. The sales team had done an excellent job at getting in touch with people after the event to find out how they were getting on and this had lead to them asking for in-house training courses and making referrals to other organizations. They had also taken photographs at the event so these could be used in future marketing – much more effective than buying stock photos.

Simon sat back and looked at what he had written. He had certainly learned a lot over the time he had been with the company and one of the people he had to thank for that was his coach Sasha. She had really helped him understand more about people, what motivates them and how to handle them. He realized that his role of Managing Director wasn't to do everything himself or even know how to do everything himself, but to direct, to be strategic and to listen. The more he had kept the lines of communication open, empowered staff to find their own solutions and focused on leading, the easier it was to stay focused. He also found his own decision-making abilities were vastly improved – because he was now clear-headed enough to think about things properly and from every angle. His sessions with Sasha were now less about her teaching him, more facilitating his thinking process and giving him time out to reflect and to plan. Simon thought that he really must write her a thank you note. He also needed to thank Karen for suggesting he have coaching. In fact, he now remembered they hadn't really moved forward on rolling out coaching to the senior management team. He made a note to speak to Karen when he got back to the office.

His mobile phone rang in his pocket. It was Angela reminding him he had a meeting in 15 minutes. He packed up his notepad and laptop and returned to the office.

There was a definite spring in his step and he was excited about the future. He already had some ideas for taking the business forward which he was keen to share with the Board when he met with them.

The next 12 months were going to be very interesting indeed.

Recipe for Getting Recommendations and Referrals

'Word of Mouth Marketing' is said to be one of the most powerful forms of marketing. When one customer recommends a product or service to another, they are trusted more than the company providing the product or service, particularly if they have not received any incentive for their endorsement.

In our experience once a customer has recommended a product to someone else or publicly given their endorsement through a testimonial, they become even more loyal to the brand. People like to be seen as consistent and sticking to their word. This means the faster people start to recommend your product to others, the more sales you are likely to make both from that customer and the ones they recommend to you.

If you can get customers to take away something they can give to their friends or ask them to 'bring a friend' next time they purchase, your customer list will grow.

Similarly if you have baked a delicious cake and served it at your dinner party, you could give your guests a doggy bag or goody bag so they can take a slice away with them. Next time you host a party, you could ask them to bring a friend along (and promise you'll serve up the cake again!).

You'll need:
Cake, napkins, gift box, ribbon, gift bag, blank greetings cards and envelopes.

Method:
Carefully wrap the cake in the napkin and place in the gift box. Tie the ribbon around the box, finishing with a bow on top – it is not enough just to hand over the taster of your product and expect your customers to give it to others. It needs to be well-presented and in a condition where it can be given to someone without any explanation. The new customer may not have had any exposure to your brand or may not currently be in the market to buy what you offer. You need to think of them as a new lead. You cannot rely on your current customers to explain what you do to them and remember all your key marketing messages. The better presented the product, the more likely the customer is to give it to others.

Hand-write a 'thank you' message in the greetings card – it is important to acknowledge and thank your customers for choosing your product. They always have a choice and having purchased in the past does not guarantee they will purchase in the future. Your competitors are working hard to lure your customers away from you. The more your customers feel valued, the more likely they are to remain loyal. Explain that the box contains a tasty gift for them. Using the word 'gift' gives the sample a value. It also plants in their mind the idea that they could in turn give it as a gift to someone else. If your sample is perishable, you need to make it clear, for example if it contains a special offer, then your customer needs to understand that it will 'spoil' at a certain date.

Place the gift box and greetings card in the gift bag. Keep out of sight and hand to each of your guests at the end of the evening as a surprise – people just love a surprise gift, so wait until your customer has purchased and is happy before handing over your 'gift' to them. This means that any feedback you get from them up until that point is genuine, rather than them feeling they need to tell you what you want to hear in order to get the free gift.

FOOD FOR THOUGHT...

Inspirational Leadership

In a previous Food for Thought we talked about culture. Inspirational leaders create a climate and a culture in which good people thrive. You will know when you have achieved this when your employees:

- Have confidence in each others' skills and abilities.
- Believe that they can count on one another ... and do.
- Hold one another to high performance standards.
- Listen to one another's ideas and opinions.
- Make it a point to publicly recognize other employees' significant contributions.
- Are comfortable admitting failure.
- Are open to ideas and suggestions from employees at every level for improving products, processes or an approach to customers.
- Honor agreements and commitments they make to each other in matters small and large.
- Provide each other – and you – with honest feedback, confident that they won't suffer recrimination

If the above happens it means that the employees are acting as if their own success is linked to that of the organization. There will be evidence of high levels of positive concern, interest and involvement in the work process throughout the organization.

FIND OUT MORE...

For more tips, tools and resources go to:
www.businesscookerybook.com/resources

Epilogue

"Prospero Año Nuevo!" "Happy New Year!" Jenny, Simon, Barbara and John clinked their glasses together as the clock struck twelve. Rosie and Noah clinked together plastic glasses holding fizzy lemonade with a splash of orange juice to make them look like champagne.

Jenny hugged John tightly and said, "Dad, I'm so glad we were able to get away for a few days to come and see you and Mum. I've really missed you both. It's not the same talking on the phone."

"We've missed you too darling," he said and drew her even closer to kiss her on the cheek. "Mum said you've been doing some wonderful things with your business."

Jenny beamed. "Mum's been amazing. She's given both of us so much help."

"I didn't realize she was helping Simon as well," he asked.

"Well, not directly, but she said some things months ago that we both thought about a lot and used in each of our businesses," she said. At that point Simon came over to hug John to wish him a Happy New Year.

"You've been looking after my little girl, then?" asked John.

"Dad..." insisted Jenny. "I am 40 now."

"No matter how grown up you are you'll always be my little girl. You might as well learn to live with it!" Jenny playfully punched him on the arm as he finished speaking.

"Yesss, I've been looking after her," Simon slurred, "and she's been looking after me too..." He winked at John. Simon wasn't used to drinking sangria, whisky and champagne in the same evening, so John didn't pass comment.

Instead John whispered to Jenny, "Something tells me he won't be up for a round of golf in the morning!"

Jenny giggled, "Has he told you about his red underpants yet?"

"No!" said John.

"He looked up Spanish New Years Eve traditions on the internet and found something that said it was traditional to wear new red underwear," they both laughed. "Thank goodness we're staying in rather than going out! Oh Dad, I forgot to tell you. Things have been going so well at Simon's company that they gave him a bonus. I'm very proud of him; he's been working so hard."

"Yes, your mum told me. So I guess he deserves a night off when no one's watching! And what's this about you taking on more staff and getting a three year contract for a chain of hotels?" John looked pleased for Jenny.

"I know! Crazy, huh?" said Jenny. "Who would have thought a year ago that things could change so much for us? Mum has been brilliant - she taught me the recipe for success, I followed it and **it worked**."

What Next?

Now go to **www.businesscookerybook.com** and register to access all the additional resources available to you. Registration is **free**.

Within the resources section you'll find more advice, tips and exercises on the topics covered in this book:

- Knowing your market
- Finding out what they want
- Making a plan
- Practicing and learning from others
- Getting the right suppliers
- Sharing the workload
- Leadership and communication
- Spreading the word
- Customer service
- Follow-up and referrals

Want more tailored assistance?
Hannah McNamara and Patrick White are experienced business coaches and trainers who work at a senior level within organizations assisting leaders with strategy and implementation.

To arrange a time to discuss your situation and the options available to you, go to **www.businesscookerybook.com/contact**